Can You Beat Ken?™

spinner books

San Francisco • Maastricht • Sydney

ACKNOWLEDGMENTS

Editor: Peter Crowell

Designer: Michelle Hill

Special thanks to Ken Jennings, Richard Levy, Suzanne Cracraft, Erin Conley, Connie Gee, Lynn Gustafson, Joe Kwong, Kirsty Melville, Jeanette Miller, and Kristen Schoen who worked so hard (and fast!) on this project.

@ 2005 Bob Moog and University Games Corporation

First edition published in 2005

spinner/books

Spinner Books, a division of

University Games Corporation
2030 Harrison Street San Francisco CA 94110

University Games Europe B.V.
Australielaan 52 6199 AA Maastricht Airport Netherlands

University Games Australia
10 Apollo Street Warriewood 2102 Australia

Library of Congress Cataloging-in Publication Data on file with the publisher

ISBN 1-57528-949-0

Printed in China

1 2 3 4 5 6 7 8 9 10 – 09 08 07 06 05

CONTENTS

FOREWORD

Utah—my home state of Utah—is the only state in the Union with an official State Cooking Pot.

This is a little-known fact. (At least I think it is. We don't put it on the license plates or anything.) And, in addition to being factual, it's novel, interesting, even sort of fun. In other words, it qualifies as trivia.

And, despite its name, I don't find trivia to be trivial at all. Sure, maybe it does you no practical good to know that Abraham Lincoln and Charles Darwin were born just hours apart, or that the giant squid has the world's largest eyes, or that Buzz Aldrin's mother's maiden name was "Moon." But that's the beauty of trivia! It's knowledge for its own sake, stripped of any messy real-world implications. It reminds you that the universe is a strange and wonderful place. Sometimes it wins bar bets. Sometimes it can win you millions of dollars on a popular American quiz show. You never know with trivia.

The State Cooking Pot of Utah, by the way, is the Dutch oven. See, aren't you glad you know that now? You never know when it might come up. I hope you enjoy the book.

Ken Jennings

INTRODUCTION

How Fast Can a Gorilla Swim?

In 1975, some 30 years ago, I entered my first trivia contest. My team was called the Anemic Sludge. We made it to the semi-finals of the 64-team Trivia Bowl at The Colorado College. My moment of glory arrived when I correctly identified Florence Bush as the hair stylist on *Leave it to Beaver*. There was cheering, applause and after the match even a few groupies appeared. I felt like a rock star for the first time in my life.

Unfortunately, that was the best I ever did in a trivia contest, but I was still hooked. I began collecting odd facts and interesting tidbits just for fun (and eventually started my own board game company, University Games). I devoured any and every trivia-based book I could find in my quest to be best, but I was missing the proverbial boat!

Trivia shouldn't be studied or collected like stamps – it is meant to be absorbed. In that sense, Ken is the ultimate sponge of trivia. For me, creating this book has been an incredible pleasure. It's allowed me to collaborate with trivia's most successful practitioner. I may not be a trivia whiz, but I'm thrilled to know one: Ken Jennings. He's the envy of all of us who never made it past the semi-finals.

Enjoy these pages, learn some new and interesting facts, and do the one thing I've never been able to do – beat Ken and place first in a game of trivia.

Happy guessing,
Bob

P.S. Gorillas can't swim.

RULES

. . . .

The Host

The player with the birthday closest to May 23rd (Ken Jennings's birthday!) is the **Host** for the first round. For one round the **Host** spins the spinner, reads the questions and keeps score. When each round ends the player to the **Host's** right becomes the next **Host**. Each round is eight questions long. A game is completed once each player serves as the **Host** one time.

Play

At the start of each round, the **Host** announces the number of points necessary to beat Ken for that round. Here's the cool part: Ken Jennings actually answered every single question in this book! We handicapped Ken by not giving him the choice on the multiple-choice questions, but he still got 75 % correct! He received 1 point for every correct answer. Ken's score appears at the top of the right hand page of each round. The answers he got wrong are printed in bold. If it's not in bold then Ken got it right.

Before reading each question, the **Host** announces to all players whether Ken answered it right or wrong. Then the **Host** spins the spinner and announces play for that question. See **Spinner Possibilities** below.

Each player (except the **Host**) answers every question. On question one, the first player to the **Host's** right goes first. On question two, the second player to the **Host's** right goes first, and so on. After everyone has answered, the **Host** announces the correct answer and notes each player's score for that round with a pencil and paper.

Winning the game

The winner is the player with the most points at the end of the game. Remember, Ken's score is indicated at the top of the right hand page of each round. The player with the most points at the end of a round (including Ken) wins that round. A game consists of the number of rounds necessary for each player (other than Ken) to serve as **Host** one time. The player with the most total points for all rounds played (including Ken) wins the game. The winner might be Ken or it might be one of the players.

Spinner Possibilities

Can You Beat Ken
The question is worth 1 point. If Ken answered incorrectly, the question is worth 2 points.

Double Value
The question is worth 2 points. If Ken answered incorrectly, the question is worth 4 points.

Underdog's Chance
When this is spun, only the player(s) in last place get to answer. The question is worth 1 point. If Ken answered incorrectly the question is worth 2 points. If everyone has the same number of points, or if the first spin of the round is an Underdog's Chance, spin again.

Gamble
All players have the option of gambling or not gambling. Gambling players bet 3 points. A correct answer gains 3 points (regardless of Ken's correct or incorrect answer). An incorrect answer loses 3 points. If a player chooses not to gamble, the question is worth 1 point regardless of Ken's correct or incorrect answer.

Can You Beat Ken?

Round 1

Questions

1. The title of Erica Jong's titillating first novel, published in 1973, is *Fear of* _____.

2. True or false? The Continental Congress and the Constitutional Convention met in Virginia.

3. What is the only planet whose day (one planetary rotation) lasts longer than its year (one orbit around the sun): Pluto, Saturn or Venus?

4. What is the first and last name of the lead guitarist in Spinal Tap, the rock group featured in the 1984 rock mockumentary?

Answers
1. *Flying*   2. False (They both met in Pennsylvania.)
3. Venus (Ken's answer: Pluto)   4. Nigel Tufnel

Can You Beat Ken?

Ken's score: 7

5. According to Mark Twain, one should "Go to Heaven for the climate, Hell for the _____."

6. True or false? William Golding wrote *Lord of the Flies*.

7. In *Seabiscuit*, what was the name of the champion horse that Seabiscuit finally defeated: General Boy, War Admiral or Trained Soldier?

8. What is the only U.S. state with no straight lines along its borders?

Answers

5. Company 6. True 7. War Admiral 8. Hawaii

Can You Beat Ken?

Round 2

Questions

1. According to Samuel Johnson, "Patriotism is the last refuge of _____."

2. True or false? Sammy Davis, Jr. never attended school and started singing and dancing in vaudeville at the age of five.

3. What region in the U.S. did the Cherokees inhabit before their forced migration in the 1830s: the Pocono Mountains, the Great Plains or Appalachia?

4. The technique of putting objects on canvas or paper is called what?

Answers

1. Scoundrels   2. True   **3. Appalachia** (Ken's answer: Florida)   4. Collage

Can You Beat Ken?

Ken's score: 6

5. In "Lose Yourself" from the movie *8 Mile*, Eminem advises: "You only get one ___, do not miss your chance to blow."

6. True or false? Established in 1732, West Virginia was the last of the original 13 colonies to be founded.

7. What year was NATO formed: 1948, 1949 or 1950?

8. What famous author sometimes writes under the names Anne Rampling and A.N. Roquelaure?

Answers

5. Shot   6. False (Georgia was the last colony founded.)
7. 1949 (Ken's answer: 1948)   8. Anne Rice

Can You Beat Ken?

Round 3

Questions

1. In "Beautiful," Christina Aguilera sings, "We are beautiful no matter what they say/Yes, _____ won't bring us down."

2. True or false? Forty-one guns are used to salute a royal birth in Great Britain.

3. What was the poker hand that Wild Bill Hickok held when he was murdered in a Deadwood saloon: a full house, a royal flush or a pair of eights and aces?

4. What is Colorado's nickname?

Answers
1. Words   2. True   3. A pair of eights and aces
4. The Centennial State (joined U.S. in 1876) (Ken's answer: Rocky Mountain State)

Can You Beat Ken?

Ken's score: 7

5. The last words of the Declaration of Independence read: " ... we mutually pledge to each other our Lives, our Fortunes and our sacred _____."

6. True or false? Montreal is Canada's most populous city.

7. Cameron Diaz made her big screen debut in what movie: *Feeling Minnesota*, *The Mask* or *There's Something About Mary*?

8. What sport begins with love and ends with a handshake?

Answers
5. Honor   6. False (Toronto is.)   7. *The Mask*   8. Tennis

Can You Beat Ken?

Round 4

Questions

1. The prestigious _____ Medal is given to the best illustrator of American children's books annually.

2. True or false? 42 degrees North latitude, which is California's northern boundary, runs through London.

3. Who was the fourth president of the United States: John Quincy Adams, James Monroe or James Madison?

4. In the 1970s TV series, who is Wonder Woman's meek alter ego?

Answers

1. Caldecott   2. False (It runs through Rome.)   3. James Madison   4. Diana Prince

Can You Beat Ken?

Ken's score: 7

5. According to Kenny Rogers's "The Gambler," "You got to know when to hold 'em, know when to fold 'em/Know when to walk away and know when to ___."

6. True or false? Martin Luther King, Jr. said, "Joy is not in things. It is in us."

7. Before it became a United States territory, did Guam belong to the Phillipines, Portugal or Spain?

8. In what New England state was the first automobile speeding ticket issued?

Answers

5. Run   6. False (Richard Wagner said it.)   7. Spain
8. Rhode Island (Ken's answer: Massachusetts)

Can You Beat Ken?

Round 5

Questions

1. According to Marilyn Monroe, "Hollywood is a place where they pay you $1,000 for a kiss and 50 cents for your _____."

2. True or false? President Coolidge was born in Vermont on the Fourth of July.

3. Who is the successful musician that composed countless movie soundtracks, including *Men in Black* and *Batman*: James Horner, Danny Elfman or Trevor Rabin?

4. In *Alice's Adventures in Wonderland*, what part of the Cheshire Cat appears first and last in his scenes?

Answers

1. Soul (Ken's answer: reputation)   2. True (July 4, 1872)
3. Danny Elfman   4. His smile suspended in the air

Can You Beat Ken?

Ken's score: 6

5. The 1969 Woodstock Festival was held at _____ _____ Farm.

6. True or false? The narrowest part of Central America can be found in Panama.

7. The shortest war on record, which lasted only thirty-eight minutes, was an 1896 conflict between Great Britain and what other country: France, Zanzibar or Spain?

8. In what U.S. state was the first chocolate bar created?

Answers

5. Max Yasgur's   6. True   **7. Zanzibar** (Ken's answer: Spain)
8. Pennsylvania (by Milton Hershey)

Can You Beat Ken?

Round 6

Questions

1. S.O.S™, tag line of the steel wool pot and pan cleansing pad, stands for, "Save our _____."

2. True or false? In the action comedy *Mystery Men*, Hank Azaria plays an amateur superhero called the Shoveller.

3. Who said, "Heaven goes by favor; if it went by merit, you would stay out and your dog would go in": Jerry Seinfeld, Mark Twain or Fran Leibowitz?

4. What working class musician from New Jersey was hailed as the "New Bob Dylan" in the early 1970s?

Answers

1. Saucepans (Ken's answer: sink)   2. False (Azaria plays the Blue Raja; William H. Macy plays the Shoveller.)   3. Mark Twain   4. Bruce Springsteen

Can You Beat Ken?

Ken's score: 6

5. _____ Diner is the setting for the 1970s sitcom, *Alice*.

6. True or false? *The Martian Chronicles* was written by Ray Bradbury.

7. Who holds the record for most rebounds in 5-, 6- and 7-game playoff series: Dennis Rodman, Wilt Chamberlain or Bill Russell?

8. What U.S. state, famous for all its mines, calls itself the Treasure State?

Answers

5. Mel's   6. True   **7. Wilt Chamberlain** (Ken's answer: Bill Russell)   8. Montana

Can You Beat Ken?

Round 7

Questions

1. The first Pokémon™ trained by Ash Ketchum was _____.

2. True or false? New York state contains the birthplaces of four of the first five U.S. presidents.

3. What '80s pop princess brought Tommy James and the Shondells' hit "I Think We're Alone Now" back to the Top 10: Tiffany, Madonna or Donna Summer?

4. What art form is Claes Oldenburg known for?

Answers
1. Pikachu   2. False (That honor belongs to Virginia.)
3. Tiffany   4. Large public sculptures

Can You Beat Ken?

Ken's score: 7

5. The lyric from Peter Gabriel's "Solsbury Hill" goes: "No one taught them _____."

6. True or false? China's Ming Dynasty reigned for more than 250 years but fell in the 10th century.

7. In which Chris Farley movie can you find him singing "Fat Guy in a Little Coat": *Tommy Boy*, *Black Sheep* or *Billy Madison*?

8. What animal has the highest brain weight to body weight ratio?

Answers
5. Etiquette (Ken's answer: manners)   6. False (It fell in the 17th century.)
7. *Tommy Boy*   8. A human being

Can You Beat Ken?

Round 8

Questions

1. On "American Idiot," Green Day sings: "Don't want to be an American idiot. One nation controlled by the _____."

2. True or false? The first postage stamp was used in 1840 in the United Kingdom.

3. Who directed *Sleepless in Seattle*: Nancy Myers, Penny Marshall or Nora Ephron?

4. Who said, "Philosophers should be kings in an ideal republic"?

Answers

1. Media   2. True   3. Nora Ephron   4. Plato

Can You Beat Ken?

Ken's score: 7

5. According to Mother Theresa, "If you judge people, you have no time to _____ them."

6. True or false? Russia and China are the only two countries covering a larger geographic area than the U.S.

7. Introduced in 1903, how many crayons did the first box of Crayolas® contain: six, eight or ten?

8. What veteran DJ was the voice of Shaggy in the *Scooby-Doo* cartoons?

Answers
5. Love (Ken's answer: hate) 6. False (Canada) 7. Eight 8. Casey Kasem

Can You Beat Ken?

Round 9

Questions

1. The last line of Alanis Morissette's hit "All I Want" is, "And all I really want is some _____."

2. True or false? Claude Monet is called the "Father of Modern Art."

3. Which is the closest to Bangladesh: the Atlantic, Indian or Pacific Ocean?

4. Who wrote the book *How to Win Friends and Influence People*?

Answers

1. Justice (Ken's answer: pizza)   2. False (Paul Cézanne is.)   3. Indian   4. Dale Carnegie

Can You Beat Ken?

Ken's score: 5

5. According to Oliver Wendell Holmes, you should " ... leave your friend to learn unpleasant things from his _____ ... "

6. True or false? Francisco de Goya's "The Third of May" can be seen in Barcelona, Spain.

7. What kind of animal is Gumby's pal Pokey: a horse, a mule or a unicorn?

8. What kind of vehicle does Ms. Frizzle drive?

Answers
5. Enemies (Ken's answer: mistakes)   6. False (It can be seen in Madrid.)   7. A horse
8. A magic school bus (Ken's answer: A jeep)

Can You Beat Ken?

Round 10

Questions

1. Robert Frost's "The Road Not Taken" ends with the lines: "I took the one less traveled by,/And that has made all the _____."

2. True or false? In 1975, Guyana achieved independence from the Netherlands.

3. During the first and only term of what U.S. president did the Great Depression begin: Calvin Coolidge, Warren Harding or Herbert Hoover?

4. Issur Danielovitch Demsky is known on the silver screen by what name?

Answers

1. Difference   2. False (Surinam achieved that independence.)
3. Herbert Hoover   4. Kirk Douglas

Can You Beat Ken?

Ken's score: 7

5. According to the "Theme from The Monkees": " ... we're too busy _____/To put anybody down."

6. True or false? In the 1944 Supreme Court case of Korematsu v. the United States, Fred Korematsu fought against the internment of Japanese-Americans.

7. Texas is the only state in the Union that has flown six flags. Which country's flag has not flown there: France, Great Britain or Spain?

8. What Native American actor became famous for his Academy Award®-nominated role in *Dances with Wolves*?

Answers

5. Singing   6. True   **7. Great Britain** (Ken's answer: France)   8. Graham Greene

Can You Beat Ken?

Round 11

Questions

1. According to Albert Einstein, one should "Learn from yesterday, live for today, hope for tomorrow. The important thing is to not stop _____."

2. True or false? Salman Rushdie was forced into hiding after release of his novel *The Satanic Verses*.

3. What empire did Genghis Khan unify: the Tartar, the Mongol or the Seljuk?

4. What founding member of The Rolling Stones died mysteriously in 1969?

Answers

1. Questioning (Ken's answer: breathing)   2. True   3. The Mongol   4. Brian Jones

Can You Beat Ken?

Ken's score: 7

5. The first lines of Outkast's "Hey Ya" are "My baby don't ____ around/Because she loves me so."

6. True or false? Tom Brokaw was the only U.S. network news anchor to be physically present at the collapse of the Berlin Wall in 1989.

7. The coats of arms presented to both Prince William and Prince Henry (Harry) of Wales featured a lion and what animal: a unicorn, a phoenix or a griffon?

8. What raspy-voiced DJ starred as himself in the 1973 classic *American Graffiti*?

Answers

5. Mess   6. True   7. A unicorn   8. Wolfman Jack

Can You Beat Ken?

Round 12

Questions

1. The official Boy Scouts of America slogan is: "Do a Good _____ Daily."

2. True or false? In the romantic comedy *13 Going on 30*, Jenna works for a fictional magazine called *Shine*.

3. On what Los Angeles street was actor Hugh Grant arrested in 1995: Sunset Blvd, Hollywood Blvd or Rodeo Drive?

4. Of the following artists, which one painted first: Picasso, Michelangelo, or Rembrandt?

Answers
1. Turn   2. False (It was called *Poise.*)
3. Sunset Blvd. (Ken's answer: Hollywood Blvd)   4. Michelangelo

Can You Beat Ken?

Ken's score: 7

5. The last verse of "America The Beautiful" begins with: "O beautiful for _____ dream/That sees beyond the years ... "

6. True or false? In the sport of skateboarding, athletes perform daffies, zudniks and helicopters.

7. Who played The Joker on the 1960s TV version of *Batman*, starring Adam West: Jack Nicholson, Cesar Romero or Frank Gorshin?

8. What is the name of the Green Hornet's alter ego?

Answers

5. Patriot   6. False (Freestyle skiing is the sport in which these are performed.)
7. Cesar Romero   8. Britt Reid

Can You Beat Ken?

Round 13

Questions

1. In Franklin Adams's poem "Baseball's Sad Lexicon," the Chicago Cubs' double play combination (1903-1910) was immortalized: "Tinker to Evers to _____."

2. True or false? Lapps are famous reindeer herders that live in northern Scandinavia.

3. What famous "Father of Texas" led the revolution against Mexico: Jim Bowie, Sam Houston or Stephen Austin?

4. What museum is home to the *Mona Lisa*?

Answers

1. Chance   2. True   3. Sam Houston   4. The Louvre

Can You Beat Ken?

Ken's score: 7

5. According to comedian Cheech Marin, "I just thought of something funny ... your _____."

6. True or false? The cape at the southern tip of Africa is called Cape Horn.

7. The Eagles wrote the song "Too Fast to Live, Too Young to Die" about what deceased pop culture icon: Marilyn Monroe, James Dean or Buddy Holly?

8. What colorful nickname has been given to Fenway Park's 37-foot left-field wall?

Answers
5. Mother (Ken's answer: face)   6. False (It's the Cape of Good Hope.)
7. James Dean   8. The Green Monster

Can You Beat Ken?

Round 14

Questions

1. The motto of the Olympics is "_____! Altius! Fortius!"

2. True or false? If you left Rio de Janeiro and sailed straight across the Atlantic, the first country you would reach would be South Africa.

3. Which pop diva reportedly insisted on a bottle of Flintstones® vitamins in her dressing room during her 2000 tour: Britney Spears, Beyoncé Knowles or Christina Aguilera?

4. How many teams start out in the NCAA Division I basketball championship tournament?

Answers
1. Citius ("Swifter! Higher! Stronger!")
2. False (You would reach Namibia.) 3. Christina Aguilera 4. 65

Can You Beat Ken?

Ken's score: 7

5. The motto of the U.S. Coast Guard is "Semper _____."

6. True or false? Alva Moog invented the electric synthesizer in the 1960s.

7. Who wrote *The Legend of Sleepy Hollow*: Nathaniel Hawthorne, Edgar Allen Poe or Washington Irving?

8. The cotton gin revolutionized the U.S. cotton industry by removing what from the cotton?

Answers
5. Paratus ("Always ready") (Ken's answer: humidis - Latin for "always wet")
6. False (It was Robert Moog.)   7. Washington Irving   8. Seeds

Can You Beat Ken?

Round 15

Questions

1. Pillsbury®'s advertising slogan is "Nothin' says lovin' like _____ from the oven."

2. True or false? The North Sea lies between England and Norway.

3. What superhero is featured on Cameron Diaz's panties in the 2000 movie *Charlie's Angels*: Wonder Woman, Spider-Man or Daredevil?

4. According to Peter, Paul and Mary, what did Puff the Magic Dragon "frolic in"?

Answers

1. Somethin'   2. True   **3. Spider-Man** (Ken's answer: Wonder Woman)
4. The autumn mist

Can You Beat Ken?

Ken's score: 7

5. According to an ad jingle, the ingredients of a McDonald's Big Mac are "Two all-beef patties, special sauce, lettuce, cheese, _____, onions on a sesame-seed bun."

6. True or false? According to the official rules of table tennis, the server must toss the ball up at least six inches from the flat of the hand before serving.

7. What king was toppled in the French Revolution: King Louis XIV, King Louis XV or King Louis XVI?

8. Which type of atom makes up most of the Earth's atmosphere and roughly 90% of the universe?

Answers

5. Pickles   6. True   7. King Louis XVI   8. Hydrogen

Can You Beat Ken?

Round 16

Questions

1. Sprite® soda's advertising slogan is "_____ your thirst."

2. True or false? Half Dome is located in Yosemite National Park.

3. What fashion designer created the pointy sequined bras worn by Madonna: Gianni Versace, Isaac Mizrahi or Jean-Paul Gaultier?

4. Which Wright brother was in the biplane for the historic first flight at Kitty Hawk, NC in 1903?

Answers

1. Obey   2. True   **3. Jean-Paul Gaultier** (Ken's answer: Isaac Mizrahi)   4. Orville

Can You Beat Ken?

Ken's score: 6

5. Cocoa Puffs® advertising slogan is "Just like a chocolate milkshake, only
   _____."

6. True or false? Topiary is the art of trimming trees or shrubs into
   ornamental shapes.

7. What year did Robert Opel streak across the stage during the Academy
   Awards®: 1972, 1974 or 1976?

8. What are the largest sharks ever known (40'-100') that lived between
   25 to 1.6 million years ago?

Answers
5. Crunchy   6. True   7. 1974   **8. Megalodons** (Ken's answer: Megasharks)

Can You Beat Ken?

Round 17

Questions

1. What group recorded the 1968 hit "Worst That Could Happen?"

2. True or false? In *Mystic River*, Sean Penn's character was a mailman.

3. The longest anyone has led the NBA in three-point shooting is two seasons. Who does not belong on this list: John Stockton, Larry Bird or Michael Adams?

4. In the 1965 film *The Sound of Music*, from what country does the von Trapp family escape?

Answers

1. The Fifth Dimension   2. False (He was a convenience store owner.)
3. John Stockton   4. Austria

Can You Beat Ken?

Ken's score: 7

5. The advertising slogan for Peter Paul's Mounds® and Almond Joy® candy bars is "Sometimes you feel like a _____, sometimes you don't."

6. True or false? According to official Major League rules, if a pitcher delays a game unnecessarily, a balk is called.

7. If you were lost in Ouagadougou, Burkina Faso, on what continent would you be: Africa, Asia or Australia?

8. What college owns the longest winning streak in Division I-A football (47 wins)?

Answers

5. Nut   6. True   7. Africa   **8. Oklahoma (1953-57)** (Ken's answer: Nebraska)

Can You Beat Ken?

Round 18

Questions

1. According to Butthead of *Beavis & Butthead*, "This sucks more than anything that has ever _____ before."

2. True or false? Virginia is the birthplace of the U.S. president who appears on the $1 bill.

3. What is Hawaiian *poi* made from: banana, coconut or taro?

4. What does the "S" in NASCAR racing stand for?

Answers
1. Sucked   2. True   3. Taro   4. Stock

Can You Beat Ken?

Ken's score: 7

5. Charlie Kaufman won a Best Original Screenplay Oscar® for *Eternal Sunshine of the _____ Mind*.

6. True or false? Bluebonnets cannot legally be picked in Texas.

7. Which of these men was born in Texas: George W. Bush, Sam Houston or Ross Perot?

8. What was the Volvo Ocean Race formerly known as?

Answers
5. *Spotless*   6. True   7. Ross Perot
8. The Whitbread Round the World Race (Ken's answer: America's Cup)

Can You Beat Ken?

Round 19

Questions

1. The opening lyrics to Wayne Newton's "Danke Schoen" are "Danke Schoen, darling, Danke Schoen/Thank you for all the ____ and pain."

2. True or false? Zebras and horses do not belong to the same zoological family.

3. Which feminist wrote *Revolution from Within*: Gloria Steinem, Germaine Greer or Betty Friedan?

4. Anna Paquin won an Oscar® for her debut film role. What was the film?

Answers

1. Joy   2. False (Both belong to Equidae.)   3. Gloria Steinem   4. *The Piano*

Can You Beat Ken?

Ken's score: 7

5. Gwen Stefani of No Doubt begins "Just A Girl" with: "Take this pink _____ off my eyes, /I'm exposed and it's no big surprise."

6. True or false? *Hejira*, or the Flight of Mohammed, the starting point of the Islamic calendar, correlates with December 25, 1 A.D. of the Gregorian calendar.

7. Which of these metals does not occur naturally: silver, copper or bronze?

8. Name the Queen rock-opera anthem lip-synched by Wayne and Garth in the 1992 movie *Wayne's World*.

Answers
5. Ribbon (Ken's answer: blindfold)   6. False (July 16, 622 A.D.)
7. Bronze   8. "Bohemian Rhapsody"

Can You Beat Ken?

Round 20

Questions

1. As Craig says in *Being John Malkovich*, "You see the world through John Malkovich's eyes. Then after about 15 minutes, you're spit out into a ditch on the side of the _____ Turnpike!"

2. True or false? Larry Bird has more NBA championship rings than Earvin "Magic" Johnson.

3. What artist painted *The Birth of Venus*: Raphael, Donatello or Botticelli?

4. On what holiday weekend is the Indianapolis 500 held?

Answers
1. New Jersey   2. False (Larry Bird, has three; Magic Johnson, has five.)
3. Botticelli   4. Memorial Day

Can You Beat Ken?

Ken's score: 7

5. Marlene Dietrich said, "A king, realizing his incompetence, can either delegate or abdicate his duties. A _____ can do neither."

6. True or false? In 1776, Captain James Cook was killed at the hands of angry Samoans.

7. Which of these countries is not a member of NATO: Lithuania, Estonia or Sweden?

8. By what process do plants convert sunlight into energy?

Answers
5. Father (Ken's answer: director)   6. False (He was killed by Hawaiians.)
7. Sweden   8. Photosynthesis

Can You Beat Ken?

Round 21

Questions

1. In the immortal words of Marcus Aurelius: "When you arise in the morning, think of what a precious privilege it is to be alive – to breathe, to think, to enjoy, to ___."

2. True or false? The only natural predators of savannah lions are warthogs.

3. Which actor has won both a Best Screenplay and Best Director Oscar®: Kevin Costner, Matt Damon or John Huston?

4. Who was the German mechanical engineer who invented and sold the first gas-powered automobile?

Answers
1. Love (Ken's answer: urinate)   2. False (Lions hunt warthogs.)
3. John Huston (Ken's answer: Matt Damon)   4. Karl Benz (1885)

Can You Beat Ken?

Ken's score: 5

5. According to Mahatma Gandhi, you should, "Live as if you were to die tomorrow. ____ as if you were to live forever."

6. True or false? "The Pension Grillparzer" is a short story set within John Irving's novel *The World According to Garp*.

7. On what legal comedy/drama did Dyan Cannon have a reccuring role as Judge Whipper Cone?

8. Radar can determine an object's distance and the direction it is traveling. What else is radar primarily used to determine?

Answers
5. Learn (Ken's answer: Love)   6. True   7. *Ally McBeal*   8. An object's speed

Can You Beat Ken?

Round 22

Questions

1. The title of Emma Lazarus's poem engraved on a tablet within the pedestal of the Statue of Liberty is entitled, "The New _____."

2. True or false? Ernest Hemingway won the Pulitzer Prize for *The Sun Also Rises*.

3. Copernicus was born in the 15th century. Galileo was born in the 16th century. In what century was Isaac Newton born: the 16th century, 17th century or 18th century?

4. According to a *Sports Illustrated* issue published in 2005, the best sports bar in America is ... ?

Answers

1. Colossus   2. False (He won it for *The Old Man and the Sea*.)
3. 17th century   **4. The Fours, Boston** (Ken's answer: Full of drunken white people)

Can You Beat Ken?

Ken's score: 6

5.   The inscription on the Liberty Bell reads: "Proclaim liberty throughout all the land unto all the _____ thereof."

6.   True or false? Diane Lane made her screen debut with Sir Laurence Olivier in the Oscar® winning film, *A Little Romance*.

7.   Who was the first to win the Grand Slam in tennis (Wimbledon, U.S., French and Australian Opens): Rod Laver, Boris Becker or Don Budge?

8.   What role did James Earl Jones play in the movie *Star Wars*, released in 1977?

Can You Beat Ken?

Round 23

Questions

1. The inscription on the wall above the statue of Abraham Lincoln at his memorial in Washington, D.C. begins with these words: "In this ____ as in the hearts of the people ... "

2. True or false? From 1930 to 1950, the Soviet Union banned table tennis because authorities believed the sport was harmful to people's eyes.

3. Which royal line was King George III, the monarch who lost the American colonies, descended from: the House of Windsor, the Hanoverians or the Stuarts?

4. According to the 23rd Psalm, "The Lord is my _____, I shall not want ... "

Answers

1. Temple (Ken's answer: chamber)   2. True
3. The Hanoverians   4. Shepherd

Can You Beat Ken?

Ken's score: 6

5. The original title page of Jonathan Swift's *Gulliver's Travels* reads: "Travels Into Several _____ Nations of the World in Four Parts by Lemuel Gulliver."

6. True or false? The French artist Seurat was the subject of the Broadway musical *Sunday in the Park with George*.

7. What disco diva sang the hit "Hot Stuff": Gloria Gaynor, Grace Jones or Donna Summer?

8. What college bowl game is called the "Granddaddy of Them All"?

Can You Beat Ken?

Round 24

Questions

1. The first three elements of the Periodic Table are hydrogen, helium and
   _____.

2. True or false? Author and utopian socialist George Orwell wrote *Brave New World* in 1932.

3. Who scored the most touchdowns (22) in his rookie season in the NFL: O.J. Simpson, Walter Payton or Gayle Sayers?

4. Written by Sun Tzu sometime in the 4th Century B.C.E., what famous book on strategy is the oldest military treatise in the world?

Answers

1. Lithium   2. False (Aldous Huxley wrote it.)
3. Gayle Sayers (Ken's answer: Walter Payton)   4. *The Art of War*

Can You Beat Ken?

Ken's score: 7

5. The jury's decision in the 1968 movie *The Producers* is "We find the defendants _____ guilty."

6. True or false? *It Happened One Night* was the first movie to win both Best Actor and Best Actress Oscars®.

7. By what title was the crown prince of France commonly known: Viscomte, Dauphin or Petit Prince?

8. What is the deepest seafloor depression in the world?

Answers

5. Incredibly   6. True (for Clark Gable and Claudette Colbert)
7. Dauphin   8. The Mariana Trench in the Pacific Ocean

Can You Beat Ken?

Round 25

Questions

1. The Lord's Prayer begins: "Our Father, who art in heaven, _____ be Thy name."

2. True or false? In John Grisham's *The Firm*, the name of the law firm is Tracher, Dixon & Mathis.

3. Where did Napoleon meet his death: Elba, St. Helena or Waterloo?

4. Name the series of children's books first published in 1963 that features the "greatest super sleuth in sneakers."

Answers

1. Hallowed   2. False (Bendini, Lambert & Locke)   3. St. Helena   4. *Encyclopedia Brown*

Can You Beat Ken?

Ken's score: 7

5.   Which Grand Slam tennis championship is played on grass?

6.   True or false? In Mel Brooks' 1987 *Star Wars* spoof, Lone Starr and Barf set off to save Planet Vespa.

7.   Naturalists have recently discovered a new creature called a saola. It resembles what known animal: a monkey, a sloth or an antelope?

8.   Who won five consecutive Wimbledon championships in 1976-1980 and shares his last name with a *Star Trek* villain?

Answers
5. Wimbledon   6. True   **7. An antelope** (Ken's answer: A sloth)   8. Bjorn Borg

Can You Beat Ken?

Round 26

Questions

1. Charles Manson's favorite Beatles song, "Helter Skelter," proclaims: "Will you, won't you want me to ____ you/I'm coming down fast but don't let me break you."

2. True or false? John Lithgow graduated *magna cum laude* from Harvard University and was a Fulbright Scholar.

3. What member of the band No Doubt is known for wearing only his underwear during most concerts: the lead guitarist, the bass player or the drummer?

4. Huang He, the Chinese name for the second longest river in China, is translated into English as what?

Answers

1. Make (Ken's answer: take)   2. True   3. The drummer   4. Yellow River

Can You Beat Ken?

Ken's score: 6

5. In "Don't Know Why," Norah Jones sings, "My heart is _____ in wine/But you'll be on my mind/Forever."

6. True or false? Mario Lemieux re-entered the NHL after a three-year retirement.

7. What is the largest country that borders Yemen: Oman, Ethiopia or Saudi Arabia?

8. The typhoon said to have saved Japan from a Mongol invasion led by Kublai Khan was called "kamikaze." What is the English translation of the word?

Answers
5. Drenched (Ken's answer: drowned)   6. True   7. Saudi Arabia   8. Divine wind

Can You Beat Ken?

Round 27

Questions

1. In "Cold Sweat," James Brown declares: "I don't care, darlin', about your faults/Huh, I just want to satisfy your ___."

2. True or false? Sam Houston, first president of the Republic of Texas and later governor of the state, was an avowed rebel who favored secession from the Union.

3. When patriot-spy Nathan Hale was caught by the British, how was he executed: by hanging, firing squad or beheading?

4. Name the British author who wrote *The Jungle Book*.

Answers
1. Pulse (Ken's answer: needs)   2. False (He was in the pro-Union minority, and so was removed from office.)   3. Hanging   4. Rudyard Kipling

Can You Beat Ken?

Ken's score: 7

5. In Queen's "Bohemian Rhapsody," Freddie Mercury sings: "Scaramouche, Scaramouche, will you do the _____?"

6. True or false? Gordy Howe's nickname is "Mr. Hockey."

7. Who was the first person to win two Nobel Prizes: Albert Einstein, Marie Curie or Linus Pauling?

8. At 52 feet below sea level, Lake Eyre is located on what continent?

Answers

5. Fandango   6. True   7. Marie Curie   8. Australia

Can You Beat Ken?

Round 28

Questions

1. In Edna St. Vincent Millay's poem entitled "Spring," she writes: "April comes like an _____, babbling and strewing flowers."

2. True or false? All cephalopods are carnivorous.

3. Which author was female: Jules Verne, E. M. Forster or George Eliot?

4. What is the tallest mountain in Greece?

Answers
1. Idiot (Ken's answer: Ophelia)   2. True   3. George Eliot   4. Mt. Olympus

Can You Beat Ken?

Ken's score: 6

5. On the White Stripes hit "Ball and Biscuit," Jack White sings: "Tell everyone in the place to just get out/we'll get _____ together ... "

6. True or false? Post-It Notes® were invented by two 3M secretaries.

7. In 1975, the rock group Aerosmith released what album: *Rock the House*, *Toys in the Attic* or *My Babe, My Toy*?

8. What is the highest waterfall in the world?

Answers

5. Clean (Ken's answer: busy)   6. False (Spencer Silver and Arthur Fry were 3M scientists.)
7. *Toys in the Attic*   8. Angel Falls (Venezuela)

Can You Beat Ken?

Round 29

Questions

1. The poet John Keats's epitaph reads: "Here lies one whose name was writ in ____."

2. True or false? Ringo Starr replaced Mitch Mitchell as the drummer for the Beatles.

3. What brand of underwear does Michael Jordan endorse: Jockey®, Fruit of the Loom® or Hanes®?

4. What president of South Korea won the 2000 Nobel Peace Prize?

Answers

1. Water   2. False (He replaced Pete Best.)   3. Hanes®   4. Kim Dae-jung

Can You Beat Ken?

Ken's score: 7

5.   The last words of heavyweight champion boxer Max Baer were, "Oh God, here I ___."

6.   True or false? In the 1987 drama *Light of Day*, Michael J. Fox jammed with 1980s rocker Pat Benatar.

7.   As of 2005, who was the youngest female to win a gold medal at the Olympics for figure skating: Peggy Fleming, Tara Lipinski or Dorothy Hamill?

8.   Name the burping drunkard in William Shakespeare's play *Twelfth Night*.

Answers
5. Go (Ken's answer: come)   6. False (Fox jammed with Joan Jett.)
7. Tara Lipinski   8. Sir Toby Belch

Can You Beat Ken?

Round 30

Questions

1. Actor John Barrymore's last words in 1942 were, "Die? I should say not, dear fellow. No Barrymore would allow such a _____ thing to happen to him."

2. True or false? Concord, MA served as one of the capitals of the fledgling U.S. before Washington, D.C. was permanently chosen.

3. What track and field star became the first American woman to win three gold medals in a single Olympics: Wilma Rudolph, Evelyn Ashford or Babe Didrikson?

4. What is the world's largest island?

Answers

1. Conventional (Ken's answer: common)   2. False
3. Wilma Rudolph (Ken's answer: Babe Didrikson)   4. Greenland

Can You Beat Ken?

Ken's score: 5

5. Abolitionist Henry Ward Beecher's last words were, "Now comes the _____."

6. True or false? The one-hit wonders, The Kingsmen, released "Wild Thing" in 1963.

7. What kind of animal were Hodori and Hosuni, the mascots of the 1988 Olympic Games in Seoul, South Korea: monkeys, tigers or bears?

8. In what state does John Grisham's legal thriller *The Partner* take place?

Answers
5. Mystery (Ken's answer: end)   6. False (They released "Louie, Louie.")
7. Tigers   8. Mississippi

Can You Beat Ken?

Round 31

Questions

1. Ludwig von Beethoven's last words were: "Friends applaud, the _____ is over."

2. True or false? Joe DiMaggio's nickname is "The Yankee Clipper."

3. Which actress made her debut in *E.T. the Extraterrestrial*: Drew Barrymore, Meg Ryan or Helen Hunt?

4. Anne Frank's diary was originally written in what language?

Answers

1. Comedy (Ken's answer: symphony)   2. True   3. Drew Barrymore   4. Dutch

Can You Beat Ken?

Ken's score: 5

5. Humphrey Bogart's last words were, "I should never have switched from Scotch to _____."

6. True or false? According to the Billiard Congress of America's official rules of 8-Ball, if one jumps the 8-ball off the table at any time, that player automatically loses.

7. What does the Hawaiian word lani mean: flower, heaven or island?

8. Paul Bryant coached 323 winning games for the University of Alabama. He is nicknamed for what mammal?

Answers

5. Martinis (Ken's answer: Gin)   6. True   **7. Heaven** (Ken's answer: island)   8. Bear

Can You Beat Ken?

Round 32

Questions

1. In *Death of a Salesman*, Arthur Miller writes, "A man's gotta _____; it comes with the territory."

2. True or false? Soprano Jenny Lind is also known as "The Swedish Nightingale."

3. What is the top speed of a Zamboni: about four mph, about nine mph or about eighteen mph?

4. What is the deepest lake in the world?

Answers
1. Dream (Ken's answer: fight)   2. True
3. About nine mph (Ken's answer: about eighteen mph)   4. Lake Baikal (in Russia)

Can You Beat Ken?

Ken's score: 4

5. Jean Harlow's famous line from the 1930 film *Hell's Angels*: "Would you be shocked if I put on something more _____?"

6. True or false? The Zambezi River is on the continent of Asia.

7. What band asked audiences to "quit playing games" on their 1996 self-titled album: *NSync, No Doubt or The Backstreet Boys?

8. What imaginary geographic line is located at 66°, 30' North latitude?

Answers
5. Comfortable   6. False (It's in Africa.)   **7. The Backstreet Boys** (Ken's answer: No Doubt)
8. Arctic Circle (Ken's answer: Tropic of Cancer)

Can You Beat Ken?

Round 33

Questions

1. In *Forrest Gump*, Tom Hanks says, "My mama always said, 'Life was like a box of _____; you never know what you're gonna get.' "

2. True or false? There are 56 signatures on the U.S. Declaration of Independence.

3. What French Post-Impressionist artist expatriated to an island in Tahiti: Vincent van Gogh, Paul Gauguin or Henri de Toulouse-Lautrec?

4. The World War I battle of Gallipoli, was an allied attempt to push through Turkey and seize what ancient city?

Answers

1. Chocolates   2. True   3. Paul Gauguin   4. Constantinople

Can You Beat Ken?

Ken's score: 7

5. In *Terminator 2: Judgment Day*, Arnold Schwarzenegger quips, "_____ la vista, baby."

6. True or false? John C. Calhoun was first elected to the U.S. Senate by write-in votes in 1954 and served 48 years.

7. Who scored the most touchdowns (six) in a single NFL game: Jim Brown, Eric Dickerson or Ernie Nevers?

8. From about 1192 until about 1868, the ruler of Japan was referred to by what title?

Answers
5. Hasta   6. False (It was Strom Thurmond.)
7. Ernie Nevers (Ken's answer: Eric Dickerson)   8. Shogun

Can You Beat Ken?

Round 34

Questions

1. In *2001: A Space Odyssey*, **HAL the Computer** says, "Dave, this _____ can serve no purpose anymore. Goodbye."

2. True or false? Poison ivy has four leaves.

3. Monte Carlo is located in what European country: Italy, Switzerland or Monaco?

4. What famous firearm innovator also contributed to the development of the typewriter?

Answers
1. Conversation   2. False (It only has three.)   3. Monaco
4. Remington (Ken's answer: Samuel Colt)

◎ 76 ◎

Can You Beat Ken?

Ken's score: 5

5. Norma Desmond's famous line in *Sunset Blvd* is "I am big. It's the
   _____ that got small."

6. True or false? A "maser" is a scientific term for microwave
   amplification by stimulated emission of radiation.

7. What late night talk show host played Joey, the baseball player Laverne
   had a crush on, in *Laverne and Shirley*: David Letterman, Jay Leno or Dick
   Cavett?

8. Where in Spain was 20th century artist Pablo Picasso born?

Answers

5. Pictures   6. True   **7. Jay Leno** (Ken's answer: David Letterman)
8. Malaga (Ken's answer: Barcelona)

Can You Beat Ken?

Round 35

Questions

1. Anthony Hopkins's famous line from *The Silence of the Lambs* is: "A census taker once tried to test me. I ate his liver with some _____ beans and a nice Chianti."

2. True or false? The jackal, like humans, has a nine-month gestation period.

3. What Australian spider has a red dot on its back: a ruby tarantula, redback spider or black recluse?

4. Who asked the musical question: "Is she really going out with him?" in 1979?

Answers

1. Fava   2. False (They gestate for two months.)

3. Redback spider (Ken's answer: black recluse)   **4. Joe Jackson** (Ken's answer: Christopher Cross)

Can You Beat Ken?

Ken's score: 6

5. In the Oliver Stone movie *Wall Street*, Michael Douglas opines: "_____, for lack of a better word, is good."

6. True or false? The speed of light is 186,282.4 miles per hour.

7. Which of these well-known mystery authors murdered a friend's mother, inspiring the film *Heavenly Creatures*: Mary Higgins Clark, Anne Perry or Agatha Christie?

8. Who said, "Candy is dandy but liquor is quicker"?

Answers

5. Greed   6. False (186,282.4 miles per SECOND)   7. Anne Perry   8. Ogden Nash

Can You Beat Ken?

Round 36

Questions

1. One of the most famous lines from *Dr. Strangelove* is: "Gentlemen, you can't fight in here. This is the ___ Room!"

2. True or false? The Jovian planets (Jupiter, Saturn, Uranus, Neptune) are composed mainly of rock.

3. Who directed the film *Play it Again, Sam* starring Woody Allen and Diane Keaton: Woody Allen, Herbert Ross or Nora Ephron?

4. Which Division I-A national championship is not decided by a tournament or playoff system?

Answers
1. War   2. False (They are composed mainly of gases.)
3. Herbert Ross (Ken's answer: Woody Allen)   4. Football

Can You Beat Ken?

Ken's score: 6

5. In *All About Eve*, Bette Davis famously warns: "Fasten your seat belts, it's going to be a _____ night."

6. True or false? *The Lion, The Witch and The Wardrobe* was written by Lewis Carroll.

7. What was William Shakespeare's first play: *Henry VI*, *The Taming of the Shrew* or *Two Gentlemen of Verona*?

8. In 1948, what famed pitcher became the oldest rookie in the history of Major League Baseball?

Answers
5. Bumpy   6. False (It was written by C.S. Lewis.)
7. *Henry VI* (Ken's answer: *Two Gentlemen of Verona*)   8. Satchel Paige

Can You Beat Ken?

Round 37

Questions

1. Marlon Brando's famous lament from *On The Waterfront*: "You don't understand! I could've had ___. I could've been a contender ... "

2. True or false? Before they were the Twins, Minnesota's Major League baseball team was the Washington Senators.

3. Who was the oldest of The Three Musketeers: Athos, Porthos or Aramis?

4. In what U.S. dependency will you find the port of Pago Pago?

Answers

1. Class (Ken's answer: everything)   2. True   3. Athos   4. American Samoa

Can You Beat Ken?

Ken's score: 7

5. In the 1967 hit *In the Heat of the Night*, Sidney Poitier uttered the memorable introductory line: "They call me Mister ____."

6. True or false? Pasteurization to remove bacteria involves heating milk to at least 131° F.

7. Who wrote *The Red Badge of Courage*: Stephen Crane, John Steinbeck or Upton Sinclair?

8. In 1823, what team sport was invented that let players carry the ball (instead of just kicking it)?

Answers
5. Tibbs   6. True   7. Stephen Crane   8. Rugby

Can You Beat Ken?

Round 38

Questions

1. When Bill Murray comments on his deathbed gift of total consciousness from the Dalai Lama in *Caddyshack*, he says, "So I got that going for me, which is ____."

2. True or false? King Richard I spent all but six months of his 10-year reign outside of England.

3. On New Year's Eve 2000, Kate Hudson married the lead singer from what band: Counting Crows, The Black Crowes or Stone the Crows?

4. Which artist created a sculpture of Michael Jackson and his pet monkey Bubbles?

Answers

1. Nice (Ken's answer: something)   2. True   3. The Black Crowes
4. Jeff Koons (Ken's answer: Tito Jackson)

Can You Beat Ken?

Ken's score: 5

5. Who fronted *The Muppet Show*'s house band, Electric Mayhem: Animal, Kermit the Frog or Dr. Teeth?

6. True or false? The European silk industry began in 553 A.D. after silkworms were smuggled out of India.

7. What was the first all-color "talkie": *Becky Sharp*, *The Jazz Singer* or *On With the Show*?

8. In what ocean are the islands of Wallis and Futuna located?

Answers
5. Dr. Teeth   6. False (They were smuggled out of China.)
7. On With the Show (Ken's answer: *Becky Sharp*)   8. The South Pacific

Can You Beat Ken?

Round 39

Questions

1. At the end of *Chinatown*, Jack Nicholson is told: "Forget it, ____, it's Chinatown."

2. True or false? Rapper and film star Ice Cube was born O'Shea Jackson.

3. A famous prehistoric painting of a bison is in a cave in Altamira in which country: France, Italy or Spain?

4. What sporting event that occurs every four years is the most-watched sporting event on Earth?

Answers

1. Jake   2. True   **3. Spain** (Ken's answer: France)   4. The World Cup (soccer)

Can You Beat Ken?

Ken's score: 7

5. In *Who Framed Roger Rabbit?*, Jessica Rabbit declares, "I'm not bad, I'm just _____ that way."

6. True or false? Richard Nixon was the first president to visit all 50 states while in office.

7. What English settlement off the coast of North Carolina vanished without a trace: Wilmington, New Stratford or Roanoke?

8. How many balls are used in a regular pocket billiards (pool) game?

Answers

5. Drawn   6. True   7. Roanoke   8. 16 (15 numbered balls, one cue ball)

Can You Beat Ken?

Round 40

Questions

1. The tagline for the 1986 movie *Ferris Bueller's Day Off* is "_____ rules."

2. True or false? George W. Bush is the first U.S. president to be the son of a previous U.S. president.

3. Sailing north from Qatar across the Persian Gulf, which country do you reach first: Iran, Saudi Arabia or Iraq?

4. In a World Championship match, a boxer is awarded how many points for winning a round?

Answers
1. Leisure (Ken's answer: Hooky)
2. False (John Quincy Adams was the son of John Adams.)   3. Iran   4. 10

Can You Beat Ken?

Ken's score: 6

5. According to cartoonist Lynda Barry: "If it is your time, love will track you down like a _____ missile."

6. True or false? Adult butterflies do not get bigger with age.

7. Africa's second longest river is located almost entirely in former Zaire. Is it the Congo, Niger or Zambezi?

8. What sentence, referring to a French dictator's exile on a small island, is a well-known palindrome?

Answers

5. Cruise (Ken's answer: guided)   6. True   7. Congo   8. "Able was I ere I saw Elba."

Can You Beat Ken?

Round 41

Questions

1. The tagline for the 1967 movie *The Graduate* explains: "This is Benjamin. He's a little _____ about his future."

2. True or false? Dizzy Gillespie, Charlie Parker and Thelonious Monk developed the bebop style of jazz in Chicago, IL.

3. How long does it take a lobster to grow to one pound: four, seven or ten years?

4. What law school did lawyer and American president Abraham Lincoln attend?

Answers

1. Worried   2. False (They developed it in New York City.)
3. Seven years (Ken's answer: ten)   4. None (He did not attend law school.)

Can You Beat Ken?

Ken's score: 7

5. The tagline for the 1973 hit *American Grafitti* asks: "Where were you in _____?"

6. True or false? Andy Warhol created the first work of Pop art in 1956.

7. Which of the following is not a birthstone: garnet, aquamarine or onyx?

8. Name the British Romantic poet who wrote, "A thing of beauty is a joy forever."

Answers

5. '62 6. False (Richard Hamilton created the first work of Pop art.) 7. Onyx 8. John Keats

Can You Beat Ken?

Round 42

Questions

1. The tagline for the 1987 screamer *The Lost Boys* is: "Sleep all day, party all night. It's fun to be a _____."

2. True or false? The Rock and Roll Hall of Fame opened in 1995 in Cleveland, OH.

3. What famous physicist and astronomer shares his name with a well-known cookie?

4. Who wrote in what is called the first "modern" novel, "A bird in the hand is worth two in the bush"?

Answers

1. Vampire   2. True   **3. Isaac Newton** (with the Fig Newton)
4. Miguel de Cervantes (Ken's answer: James Joyce)

Can You Beat Ken?

Ken's score: 6

5. George Orwell's prophetic novel, *1984*, opens with: "It was a bright cold day in April, and the clocks were striking _____."

6. True or false? *In Mars Attacks!*, the only way to kill the evil Martians is to play Slim Whitman songs.

7. If stung by an Australian sea wasp, a person has how long to live: three minutes, three hours or three days?

8. Within 10, how many paintings did Vincent van Gogh sell in his lifetime?

Answers

5. Thirteen   6. True   7. Three minutes   8. One (Zero-11 counts as a correct answer.)

Can You Beat Ken?

Round 43

Questions

1. According to legendary Green Bay Packers coach Vince Lombardi, "Winning is not everything. It's the ____ thing."

2. True or false? The writer with the most books adapted for the silver screen is Stephen King.

3. Which is the strongest metal in the world: iron, tungsten or titanium?

4. How many brains does a starfish have?

Can You Beat Ken?

Ken's score: 5

5. According to the Greek philosopher Plato, "You can discover more about a person in an hour of _____ than in a year of conversation."

6. True or false? Orson Welles was the first actor to ever direct himself in an Academy Award®-winning performance.

7. What is Lady Bird Johnson's real first name?

8. What big band leader and accomplished scat singer is best known for his 1931 hit "Minnie the Moocher"?

Answers

5. Play (Ken's answer: observation)   6. False (Laurence Olivier was the first.)
7. Claudia   8. Cab Calloway

Can You Beat Ken?

Round 44

Questions

1. According to Yankee great Yogi Berra, "Baseball is 90% mental, the other ____ is physical."

2. True or false? Michael Jordan was the first non-center in the NBA to win three consecutive MVP awards.

3. What is the middle name of A.A. Milne, the author of *Winnie-the-Pooh*: Alan, Alexander or Aubrey?

4. What was the name of the first dog in space, sent by the Russians in November 1957?

Answers

1. Half   2. False (Larry Bird, '84-'86)   3. Alexander   4. Laika (aka "Muttnik")

Can You Beat Ken?

Ken's score: 7

5. According to William Shakespeare, "Neither a _____ nor a lender be."

6. True or false? Dom, Vince and Joe DiMaggio are the first siblings to play all three outfield positions at the same time in a major league baseball game.

7. What is Charlotte Brontë's pen name: Currer Bell, Edna St. Vincent Millay or Francine du Plessix?

8. At the Massasoit Convention of 1876, the rules for what major sport were written?

Answers

5. Borrower   6. False (S.F. Giants' Felipe, Jesus and Matty Alou all appeared in the outfield on September 15, 1963. The DiMaggios never did.)   7. Currer Bell   **8. American Football** (Ken's answer: Baseball)

Can You Beat Ken?

Round 45

Questions

1. In *Casablanca*, Humphrey Bogart says, "Of all the ____ joints in all the towns in all the world, she walks into mine."

2. True or false? President Warren G. Harding died at the Palace Hotel in San Francisco, CA.

3. Which artist was born first: Michelangelo, Jan van Eyck or Hieronymus Bosch?

4. Which former member of the band The Wailers was gunned down in his home during a robbery in 1987?

Answers

1. Gin   2. True   3. Jan van Eyck (1395)   **4. Peter Tosh** (Ken's answer: Ziggy Marley)

Can You Beat Ken?

Ken's score: 6

5. Aladdin and his lamp are key figures in the collection of tales known as *A Thousand and One _____*.

6. What 1984 film starring Rob Lowe and Jodie Foster features Natassja Kinski in a bear suit: *Weird Science, The Hotel New Hampshire* or *Fandango*?

7. Who wrote *Beloved*: Maya Angelou, Toni Morrison or Alice Walker?

8. What did San Francisco 49ers safety Ronnie Lott remove so he could play football?

Answers
5. *Nights*   6. *The Hotel New Hampshire*   7. Toni Morrison
8. Part of his little finger (Ken's answer: Front teeth)

Can You Beat Ken?

Round 46

Questions

1. Stanley Kubrick's *A Clockwork Orange* begins with Alex saying, "There was me, that is Alex, and my three _____, that is Pete, Georgie, and Dim ... "

2. True or false? The U.S. military used Hopi smoke signals as an unbreakable code during World War II.

3. Which actor played Genghis Khan in the 1956 film *The Conqueror*: John Wayne, Toshiro Mifune or Yul Brynner?

4. What Major League Baseball team won the World Series in 2003, the 100th anniversary of the first Series?

Answers

1. Droogs   2. False (They used the Navajo language.)   3. John Wayne   4. The Florida Marlins

Can You Beat Ken?

Ken's score: 7

5. The first line of Francis Coppola's *The Godfather* is: "I believe in _____."

6. True or false? The first James Bond™ novel that Ian Fleming wrote was *Dr. No*.

7. Element 102, the last of the actinoid group and found at the bottom of the Periodic Table is _____.

8. What were the names of the Siamese twins made famous by P.T. Barnum?

Answers

5. America   6. False (It was *Casino Royale.*)
7. Nobelium (No) (Ken's answer: Californium)   8. Chang and Eng

Can You Beat Ken?

Round 47

Questions

1. At the end of Frank Capra's *It's a Wonderful Life*, Zuzu Bailey says, "Look, Daddy. Teacher says, every time a bell rings, an ____ gets his wings."

2. True or false? Wood is the traditional gift for a couple's fifth wedding anniversary.

3. Who played Agent 99 on *Get Smart*: Barbara Eden, Barbara Feldon or Elizabeth Montgomery?

4. Who is considered to be the mother of the birth control movement?

Answers

1. Angel   2. True   3. Barbara Feldon   4. Margaret Sanger

Can You Beat Ken?

Ken's score: 7

5. Broadcast in 1953, *The War of the Worlds* ends with: "After all that men could do had failed, the _____ were destroyed and humanity saved ... "

6. True or false? George Clooney portrayed Batman in 1995's *Batman Forever*.

7. Who played Audrey Hepburn's Asian neighbor in *Breakfast at Tiffany's*: Anna May Wong, James Hong or Mickey Rooney?

8. What civil rights activist died in Guinea under the name Kwame Toure in 1998?

Answers
5. Martians   6. False (Val Kilmer did.)   7. Mickey Rooney
8. Stokely Carmichael (Ken's answer: Eldridge Cleaver)

Can You Beat Ken?

Round 48

Questions

1. At the end of *My Fair Lady*, Rex Harrison says to Audrey Hepburn: "Eliza? Where the devil are my _____?"

2. True or false? Gloria Steinem and Sylvia Plath are both alumnae of Smith College.

3. Who turned down a lead role in *The Matrix* and won the first Grammy given for rap: DJ Jazzy Jeff, Will Smith or LL Cool J?

4. What silent movie actress was known as the "It Girl" and defined the Roaring '20s?

Answers

1. Slippers   2. True   3. Will Smith   4. Clara Bow

Can You Beat Ken?

Ken's score: 7

5. At the end of *Planet of the Apes*, released in 1968, Charlton Heston rails: "You finally really did it. You _____! You blew it up! God damn you! God damn you all to hell!"

6. True or false? The Librarian of Congress appoints the U.S. Poet Laureate.

7. In 1987, what rock band became the first band since the Who to appear on the cover of *Time Magazine*: Nirvana, U2 or The Clash?

8. Who was the first Jewish U.S. Supreme Court Justice?

Answers
5. Maniacs (Ken's answer: idiots)   6. True   7. U2   8. Louis Brandeis

Can You Beat Ken?

Round 49

Questions

1. As Woody Allen tells Diane Keaton in *Annie Hall*, "I have a very pessimistic view of life ... I feel that life is divided up into the horrible and the _____."

2. True or false? K2 is the world's second-highest mountain.

3. Is the yellow track suit that Uma Thurman wears in *Kill Bill* a direct tribute to: Carl Lewis, Foxy Brown or Bruce Lee?

4. What artist used the blank advertising panels in New York City's subway stations as a canvas and died of an AIDS-related illness in 1990?

Answers
1. Miserable (Ken's answer: terrible)   2. True
3. Bruce Lee   **4. Keith Haring** (Ken's answer: Basquiat)

Can You Beat Ken?

Ken's score: 6

5. As Crash Davis muses in *Bull Durham*: " ... I believe in long, slow, deep, soft, wet kisses that last _____ days."

6. True or false? The first paperback book appeared in New York in 1938.

7. What are they in search of in *The Hunt for Red October*: a Soviet submarine, a Soviet jet or a Soviet nuclear bomb?

8. For which novel did Ernest Hemingway win the Pulitzer Prize?

Answers

5. Three   6. False (It appeared in England.)   7. A Soviet submarine
8. *The Old Man and the Sea*

Can You Beat Ken?

Round 50

Questions

1. What was the name of the darling little teacup in *Beauty and the Beast*?

2. True or false? Underdog had a crush on TV reporter Penelope Pitstop.

3. Who said, "Men are creatures with eight hands": Gloria Steinem, Jayne Mansfield or Doris Day?

4. Who wrote the *Curious George* series?

Answers
1. Chip   **2. False** (Her name was Sweet Polly Purebread.)
3. Jayne Mansfield (Ken's answer: Gloria Steinem)   4. H.A. Rey

◎ 108 ◎

Can You Beat Ken?

Ken's score: 5

5. According to comic strip artist Cathy Guisewite: "Food, love, career and mothers, the four major _____ groups."

6. True or false? In the 19th century, Zachary Taylor was the leader of the Democratic Party.

7. What technological innovation was invented in Mainz, Germany, in the 15th century: the tin can, the iron plow or the Gutenberg press?

8. What English baroness and politician was known as the Iron Lady in the Soviet Union?

Answers
5. Guilt (Ken's answer: anxiety)   6. False (He was leader of the Whig Party.)
7. The Gutenberg press   8. Margaret Thatcher

Can You Beat Ken?

Round 51

Questions

1. Friedrich Nietzsche philosophized, "That which does not kill me makes me
    _____."

2. True or false? Elephants have the largest eyes of any land mammal.

3. How many stomachs does a cow have: four, one or three?

4. In volleyball, what do you call the player who hits the ball up in the air so a
    teammate can spike it?

Answers

1. Stronger   2. False (Giraffes have the largest eyes.)   3. Four   4. A setter

Can You Beat Ken?

Ken's score: 6

5. Scout's narration in the movie *To Kill A Mockingbird* begins with: "_____ was a tired old town, even in 1932 when I first knew it."

6. True or false? Vivaldi's *Four Seasons* is a concerto written for the flute.

7. Roughly how many residents did the American colonies have in 1770: 1,000,000; 2,000,000 or 20,000,000?

8. What is the name of the resort in Stephen King's novel *The Shining*?

Answers

5. Maycomb   6. False (It was written for the violin.)   **7. 2,000,000** (Ken's answer: 1,000,000)
8. The Overlook Hotel (Ken's answer: The Moose Jaw Hotel)

Can You Beat Ken?

Round 52

Questions

1. For the daughter of what U.S. president is the Baby Ruth candy bar named?

2. True or false? Benazir Bhutto was the first woman to rule a predominantly Muslim country.

3. Which Scandinavian country's symbol is three crowns: Denmark, Sweden or Finland?

4. What was John Calvin's native language?

Answers
1. Grover Cleveland   2. True   **3. Sweden** (Ken's answer: Finland)   4. French

Can You Beat Ken?

Ken's score: 7

5. In 1964, Malcolm X began his "The Ballot or the Bullet" speech with: "Brothers and sisters, friends and _____ ... "

6. True or false? Soccer player Edson Arantes do Nascimento of Brazil is considered to be the greatest soccer player in history.

7. On what Jane Austen novel is the movie *Clueless* loosely based?

8. What did the Dodgers do to the Yankees in 1955, 1963 and 1981?

Answers
5. Enemies   6. True   (aka Pelé)   7. *Emma*
8. Beat them in the World Series.

Can You Beat Ken?

Round 53

Questions

1. In "London's Burning," the Clash sing: "Black or white turn it on, face the new _____/Everybody's sitting 'round watching television!"

2. True or false? In every major U.S. war, the Marines have sustained the most casualties.

3. What South American country boasts Nobel Prize-winning poet Pablo Neruda as a native son: Chile, Paraguay or Ecuador?

4. At age nineteen, George Foreman won an Olympic gold medal in boxing. Within five years, how old was he when he won his second heavyweight boxing title?

Answers

1. Religion (Ken's answer: decision)   2. False (The Army has.)
3. Chile   4. 45 (Forty to fifty count as a correct answer.)

Can You Beat Ken?

Ken's score: 6

5. According to the Bible, "It is easier for a ____ to pass through the eye of the needle than for a rich man to enter the Kingdom of God."

6. True or false? One pound of honey equals the life work of approximately 300 bees and a flight distance of two to three times around the earth.

7. In what Rudyard Kipling book did Rikki-Tikki Tavi appear: *Gunga Din*, *The Jungle Book* or *Kim*?

8. What are the stretches of DNA that have no known function called?

Answers

5. Camel   6. True   7. *The Jungle Book*   **8. Junk DNA** (Ken's answer: Blank sequences)

Can You Beat Ken?

Round 54

Questions

1. In 1987, President Ronald Reagan said at the Brandenburg Gate: "Mr. Gorbachev, tear down this ____!"

2. True or false? In the 1999 comedy *Dogma*, Janeane Garofolo played God.

3. Was Michelangelo's last name: Buonarroti, Domenico or De Giovanni?

4. What country crooner had a crossover hit with 1975's "Rhinestone Cowboy"?

Answers

1. Wall   2. False (Alanis Morissette played God.)   3. Buonarroti
4. Glen Campbell (Ken's answer: Willie Nelson)

Can You Beat Ken?

Ken's score: 6

5. Winston Churchill defined a fanatic as one who "can't change his mind and won't change the _____."

6. True or false? In 1953, golfing legend Ben Hogan won the Masters, the U.S. Open and the British Open.

7. The concert film *Rattle and Hum* features which band: The Who, U2 or Simon *&* Garfunkel?

8. Archie Griffin, the only two-time winner of the Heisman trophy, played for what Big Ten school?

Answers

5. Subject   6. True   7. U2   **8. Ohio State** (Ken's answer: Nebraska)

Can You Beat Ken?

Round 55

Questions

1. In their 1975 hit, the Captain and Tennille sang to each other: "Love will keep us_____."

2. True or false? Alexander Hamilton is the only non-President who appears on U.S. paper money worth less then $50.

3. Who sculpted the goat in the sculpture garden at the New York MOMA: Rodin, Calder or Picasso?

4. What endangered bird is often spotted in debates between loggers and conservationists in the Pacific Northwest?

Answers

1. Together   2. True   **3. Picasso** (Ken's answer: Rodin)   4. The spotted owl

Can You Beat Ken?

Ken's score: 6

5. In the Rolling Stones' song "Wild Horses," Mick Jagger sings: "Faith has been broken, tears must be cried/Let's do some living, _____ we die."

6. True or false? Billie Jean King's first Wimbledon title came as a doubles player. It would be five more years (1966) before she won a singles championship there.

7. What "brand new dance" was Little Eva teaching people how to do in 1962: the Locomotion, the Twist or the Mashed Potato?

8. What 16th century Polish astronomer, mathematician and economist is famous for postulating the revolutionary idea of a heliocentric solar system?

Answers

5. After (Ken's answer: tomorrow)   6. True
7. The Locomotion   8. Nicolaus Copernicus

Can You Beat Ken?

Round 56

Questions

1. U2's anthem "Sunday, Bloody Sunday" begins with Bono singing: "I can't believe the _____ today."

2. True or False: The largest recorded spider in the world was a tarantula whose legs spanned nearly 13 inches.

3. Which actor portrayed the heroic Wesley in the fantasy film *The Princess Bride*: Christopher Guest, Cary Elwes or Kenneth Branagh?

4. What is the name of the building, once a mecca of the 1960s music industry, located at 1619 Broadway in New York City?

Answers
1. News   **2. True**   3. Cary Elwes   4. The Brill Building

Can You Beat Ken?

Ken's score: 6

5. The heroine of *Annie* sings in her show-stopper, "Just thinkin' about tomorrow/Clears away the _____ and the sorrow ... "

6. True or false? *Chinatown* is the story of how water was brought to San Francisco, CA.

7. What type of currency was used during the reign of Kublai Khan: diamonds, paper or gold?

8. What famous journey occurred during the night of April 18, 1775?

Answers

5. Cobwebs   6. False (It refers to Los Angeles, CA.)   **7. Paper** (Ken's answer: Diamonds)
8. The midnight ride of Paul Revere

Can You Beat Ken?

Round 57

Questions

1. The Executive Oath of Office recited by every American president states: "I ... will, to the best of my ability, preserve, protect and defend the _____ of the United States."

2. True or false? Mosaics are an ancient art form going back nearly 5,000 years. The world's largest mosaic can be found in Athens, Greece.

3. Cy Young holds the record for most innings pitched in a career. How many is it: 5,280; 7,356 or 12,571?

4. Before directing the anti-war classic *Coming Home*, who edited such films as *The Cincinnati Kid* and *The Thomas Crown Affair*?

Answers

1. Constitution   2. False (The world's largest mosaic is found in Mexico City, Mexico.)
3. 7,356   **4. Hal Ashby** (Ken's answer: John Avildsen)

Can You Beat Ken?

Ken's score: 6

5. When Marion notes how Indiana Jones has aged in *Raiders of the Lost Ark*, he says: "It's not the years, honey, it's the _____."

6. True or false? Peter, Paul and Mary's only #1 hit, "Leaving on a Jet Plane," was actually written by John Denver.

7. New Orleans is more famous for it, but which state further east held the first Mardi Gras in America: Mississippi, Alabama or Florida?

8. What is the Solar System's second largest planet, which is light enough to float in water?

Answers

5. Mileage   6. True   **7. Alabama** (Ken's answer: Florida)   8. Saturn

Can You Beat Ken?

Round 58

Questions

1. According to Albert Einstein, "_____ equals mass times the speed of light squared."

2. True or false? The Athenians lost to the Spartans in the Peloponnesian War.

3. A shark's teeth are actually modified what: gums, bone or scales ?

4. Who sculpted *The Thinker* and *The Crouching Woman*?

Answers
1. Energy   2. True   **3. Scales** (Ken's answer: gums)   4. Auguste Rodin

Can You Beat Ken?

Ken's score: 6

5. Kermit the Frog believes, "Time's fun when you're having ____."

6. True or false? Hippos excrete a red liquid from their pores, which protects their skin from sun and infection.

7. Which of these sets of sex chromosomes produces a female child: XX, XY or YY?

8. Catherine of Aragon's first husband was what relation to her future husband, Henry VIII?

Answers

5. Flies   6. True   7. XX   **8. Brother** (Ken's answer: cousin)

Can You Beat Ken?

Round 59

Questions

1. David Lean's *Lawrence of Arabia* opens with the line: "He was the most _____ man I ever knew."

2. True or false? In the 1967 song "San Francisco," Scott McKenzie advises listeners to wear peasant shirts.

3. What is the average temperature on Venus: 900° F, 100° F or -100° F?

4. What active Sicilian volcano still spews ash and lava, holding the attention of the residents below?

Answers

1. Extraordinary (Ken's answer: remarkable)   2. False (He tells them to wear flowers.)
3. 900° F (Ken's answer: 100° F)   4. Mount Etna

Can You Beat Ken?

Ken's score: 5

5. When Maria sings "The Sound of Music," she yearns: "To sing through the night, like a _____ who is learning to pray."

6. True or false? Comic actor Gene Wilder co-wrote the movie *Young Frankenstein* with Mel Brooks.

7. What is the subject of Robert Mitchum's epic *Thunder Road*: bootlegging, auto racing or World War II?

8. What 1978 movie, starring Tatum O'Neal, was a sequel to the 1944 classic *National Velvet*?

Answers

5. Lark   6. True   **7. Bootlegging** (Ken's answer: World War II)   8. *International Velvet*

Can You Beat Ken?

Round 60

Questions

1. The Who's hit song "Won't Get Fooled Again" finishes with: "Meet the new boss/___ as the old boss."

2. True or false? Jonathan Lipnicki played Ray Boyd in *Jerry McGuire*.

3. What kind of paintings are Michelangelo's Sistine Chapel masterpieces: impastos, landscapes or frescoes?

4. With 36 wins, France has the most Tour de France titles. What neighboring nation comes in second with 18?

Answers

1. Same   2. True   3. Frescoes   **4. Belgium** (Ken's answer: Spain)

Can You Beat Ken?

Ken's score: 6

5. Robert Burns' poem "A Red, Red Rose" begins: "O, my Luve's like a red, red rose,/That's newly sprung in _____."

6. True or false? Determining the sex of a spotted hyena is quite difficult as the male and female sexual organs have a very similar appearance.

7. The world's first civilizations appeared around 5,000 B.C. Which of the following was not one of them: Sumerian, Babylonian or Phoenician?

8. The coccyx, located at the base of the human spine, is thought by some to be the evolutionary remainder of what body part?

Answers
5. June (Ken's answer: May)   6. True   7. Phoenicians   8. A tail

Can You Beat Ken?

Round 61

Questions

1. What fitness expert is also the author of nine books, including the *New York Times* best seller *Never Say Diet*?

2. True or false? The French sustained more casualties among soldiers during World War I than World War II.

3. In 1879, Detroit, MI was the first city to assign what numbers to help its residents: phone numbers, zip codes or street addresses?

4. What was the first English colony founded in what is now the United States?

Answers

1. Richard Simmons   2. True   **3. Phone numbers** (Ken's answer: street addresses)
4. Roanoke Colony (Ken's answer: Jamestown)

Can You Beat Ken?

Ken's score: 5

5. According to actress Ingrid Bergman: "Happiness is good health and a bad _____."

6. True or false? The first transcontinental airmail route was established in 1920.

7. The "49ers" were looking for gold in the foothills of what mountain range: Rockies, Coast Range or Sierra Nevada?

8. What is the more famous name of the Maid of Orléans?

Answers

5. Memory (Ken's answer: diet)   6. True   7. Sierra Nevada   8. Joan of Arc

Can You Beat Ken?

Round 62

Questions

1. Dorothy Parker once said, "Men seldom make passes at girls who wear
   _____."

2. True or false? Jon Scieszka wrote a Mother Goose parody called *If You Give a Bear a Bun*.

3. Who was the first African-American justice of the U.S. Supreme Court: Clarence Thomas, Thurgood Marshall or Frederick Douglass?

4. What famous Russian was also known as the Mad Monk?

Answers

1. Glasses   **2. False** (It was called *The Stinky Cheese Man*.)   3. Thurgood Marshall   4. Rasputin

Can You Beat Ken?

Ken's score: 5

5. In the film *Cool Hand Luke*, the prison warden says with frustration, "What we have here is a failure to _____."

6. True or false? Singer Björk hails from Iceland.

7. Who was the first woman prime minister in the world: Sirimavo Bandaranaike, Margaret Thatcher or Golda Meir?

8. Name the German who invented an internal combustion engine in 1892 and published a paper called "The Theory and Construction of a Rational Heat Engine."

Answers

5. Communicate   6. True   **7. Sirimavo Bandaranaike** (Ken's answer: Golda Meir)
8. Rudolf Diesel (Ken's answer: Carnot)

Can You Beat Ken?

Round 63

Questions

1. Oscar Wilde said sincerely, "A little sincerity is a dangerous thing, and a great deal of it is absolutely _____."

2. True or false? J.D. Salinger's initials stand for Jerome David.

3. Which expatriate in Paris coined the term the Lost Generation: Gertrude Stein, Alice B. Toklas or Henry Miller?

4. What Indian Prime Minister was assassinated by her own bodyguards after ordering a military attack on the holiest shrine of the Sikh religion?

Answers

1. Fatal (Ken's answer: dull)   2. True   3. Gertrude Stein   4. Indira Gandhi

Can You Beat Ken?

Ken's score: 5

5. Helen Keller, born blind and mute, once said: "Security is mostly a
_____. It does not occur in nature."

6. True or false? In 1975, Fred Lynn of the Boston Red Sox was both the
Rookie of the Year and the American League MVP.

7. Which city was the capital of the Confederacy during most of the Civil
War: Richmond, Montgomery or Gettysburg?

8. What sports league's first All-Star tournament, held in 1999, was kicked
off with the national anthem sung by Whitney Houston?

Answers
5. Superstition (Ken's answer: lie)   6. True
7. Richmond (Ken's answer: Montgomery)   8. The WNBA

Can You Beat Ken?

Round 64

Questions

1. Martin Luther King, Jr. closed his "I Have a Dream" speech with: "Thank God almighty, we are ____ at last."

2. True or false? John Kennedy Toole won the Pulitzer Prize posthumously for *A Confederacy of Dunces*.

3. How many quarter-pound hamburgers can be made from an average cow: 40, 400 or 4,000?

4. At 1,332 feet at its deepest, and an average depth of 500 feet, which is the deepest of the Great Lakes?

Answers

1. Free   2. True   **3. 400** (Ken's answer: 4,000)   4. Lake Superior

Can You Beat Ken?

Ken's score: 6

5. The first article of the U.S. Constitution reads, "All _____ Powers herein granted shall be vested in a Congress of the United States ... "

6. True or false? The 17th century was the golden age for Baroque art.

7. Which state seceded from England before the Declaration of Independence was signed: Vermont, Massachusetts or New Hampshire?

8. Cuban Olympian Teofilo Stevenson won three gold medals in what sport?

Answers

5. Legislative   6. True   **7. New Hampshire** (Ken's answer: Massachusetts)   8. Boxing

Can You Beat Ken?

Round 65

Questions

1. In the first verse of "Hello, Dolly!" the chorus sings, "Dolly, you're still glowin',/you're still _____,/you're still goin' strong."

2. True or false? In the famous painting by Emanuel Leutze, George Washington's boat is crossing the Delaware River.

3. Historians point to the attack in 410 A.D. as the start of the collapse of Rome. Who led the assault: Attila the Hun, Alaric the Goth or Genghis Khan?

4. The U.S. Viking probe was the first spacecraft to reach Mars. During which decade did Viking reach Mars?

Answers
1. Crowin' (Ken's answer: growin')   2. True
3. Alaric the Goth (Ken's answer: Attila the Hun)   4. The 1970s (1976)

Can You Beat Ken?

Ken's score: 5

5. At the very end of "Satisfy You" on his CD *Forever*, P. Diddy raps, "This one right here goes out to all my _____."

6. True or false? Two-time Academy Award®-nominated Charles Durning plays the role of evil Doc Hopper in *The Muppet Movie*.

7. Delaware calls itself the first state. What did Delaware do first: sign the Declaration of Independence, stop paying taxes or ratify the Constitution?

8. Uranus takes roughly 84 years to orbit the Sun, and Pluto takes 249 years. Within 20 years, how many years does Neptune take?

Answers

5. Sisters (Ken's answer: playas)   6. True   7. Ratify the Constitution
8. 164 (144-184 is considered a correct answer.)

Can You Beat Ken?

Round 66

Questions

1. The opening title card of Sergei Eisenstein's *Battleship Potemkin* reads: "_____ is the only lawful, equal, effectual war."

2. True or false? Thomas Jefferson co-authored *The Federalist Papers* and is known as the "Father of the Constitution."

3. Who won the 1947 Pulitzer Prize for *All the King's Men*: Jack Armstrong, Robert Penn Warren or E.B. White?

4. What championship baseball team was nicknamed the Big Red Machine in the 1970s?

Answers

1. Revolution   2. False (James Madison is.)
3. Robert Penn Warren   **4. The Cincinnati Reds** (Ken's answer: The Cardinals)

Can You Beat Ken?

Ken's score: 5

5. On his hit "If I Want To," Usher opens the song with, "Every time I look up/I see it in your face/You wanna ___ up with me."

6. True or false? Peggy Fleming won two consecutive Olympic gold medals for figure skating.

7. Who painted *The Scream* in 1893: Edvard Munch, Claude Monet or Edouard Manet?

8. In 1783, John Michell first put forth the idea of the galactic phenomenon that later became known as what?

Answers

5. Hook (Ken's answer: come)   6. False (She only won one, in 1968.)
7. Edvard Munch   **8. Black Hole** (Ken's answer: The Big Bang)

Can You Beat Ken?

Round 67

Questions

1. The opening line of *On The Waterfront* is, "Joey, Joey Doyle! ... Hey, I got one of your _____."

2. True or false? The Egytian symbol of a snake corresponds to the letter J in the alphabet.

3. Who holds the record for most baseball games played (3,562), most at-bats (14,053) and most hits (4,256): Babe Ruth, Pete Rose or Cal Ripken, Jr.?

4. What country provides the Caspian Sea with its southernmost shore?

Answers
1. Birds (Ken's answer: pigeons)   2. True   3. Pete Rose   4. Iran

Can You Beat Ken?

Ken's score: 6

5. The opening sentence of Herman Melville's *Moby Dick* is, "Call me
    _____."

6. True or false? In the 19th century the Know-Nothings and the
    Mugwumps were very politically active in the U.S.

7. What speed of winds defines a category four storm: 75-100 mph,
    100-135 mph or 131-155 mph?

8. On what island will you find the city of Denpasar?

Answers

5. Ishmael   6. True   7. 100-135 mph   **8. Bali** (Ken's answer: Borneo)

Can You Beat Ken?

Round 68

Questions

1. Rudyard Kipling's oft-recited poem entitled "Gunga Din" ends with the lines: "You're a _____ man than I am, Gunga Din!"

2. True or false? Friedrich Nietzsche was very influential in early American political thought.

3. Why did Leonardo da Vinci paint *The Last Supper*: the Pope asked him, his patron paid him or he loved painting?

4. The New York Yankees' Leo Durocher was loud, cocky and talkative. What facial feature provides his nickname?

Answers

1. Better   2. False (He wasn't, but John Locke was.)

3. His patron paid him. (Ken's answer: The Pope asked him.)   4. The lips (Leo the Lip)

Can You Beat Ken?

Ken's score: 5

5. Carl Sandburg's "Fog" begins with the stanza: "The fog comes/on little ___ feet."

6. True or false? Chile is only 250 miles wide but stretches over 2,500 miles north to south.

7. What creates fjords: wind, glaciers or volcanic activity?

8. How many feet above sea level is the Indian Ocean?

Answers
5. Cat   6. True   **7. Glaciers** (Ken's answer: volcanic activity)
8. Zero feet (Ken's answer: 10 feet)

Can You Beat Ken?

Round 69

Questions

1. In his first inaugural address, Abraham Lincoln closed with, "The ____ chords of memory, stretching from every battlefield and patriot grave ... "

2. True or false? X is the only letter of the alphabet that is not used to start the name of a country.

3. Who has scored the most goals (92) in a single NHL season: Wayne Gretzky, Bobby Orr or Mario Lemieux?

4. Who is the author of *The Hotel New Hampshire* and *The World According to Garp*?

Answers
1. Mystic (Ken's answer: somber)   2. True   3. Wayne Gretzky   4. John Irving

Can You Beat Ken?

Ken's score: 6

5. In George Orwell's *Animal Farm*, Napoleon the pig says, "All animals are equal, but some animals are more _____ than others."

6. True or false? The two main ethnic groups on the Mediterranean island of Cyprus are the Greeks and the Turks.

7. Where do 70% of all the almonds eaten in the world come from: California, India or Egypt?

8. Which female painter's self-portraits feature prominent eyebrows?

Answers
5. Equal   6. True   **7. California** (Ken's answer: India)   8. Frida Kahlo

Can You Beat Ken?

Round 70

Questions

1. Alexander Pope once said, "A little learning is a _____ thing."

2. True or false? Russia sold Alaska to the U.S. in an 1867 transaction that would become known as Seward's Folly.

3. Dave Williams was hit with the most penalty minutes of any NHL player. How many minutes did that amount to: 1,785, 2,783 or 3,966?

4. What gland releases digestive enzymes and helps regulate our sugar (or insulin) intake?

Answers

1. Dangerous   **2. True**   3. 3,966   4. The pancreas

Can You Beat Ken?

Ken's score: 6

5. In his Declaration of War on Japan, Franklin D. Roosevelt began with, "Yesterday, December 7, 1941 – a date which will live in _____ ... "

6. True or false? Booker T. Washington was a famous educator.

7. How many Super Bowls did Joe Montana win for the San Francisco 49ers: three, four or five?

8. What is Liberia's capital, named after the fifth U.S. president by freed slaves: Monrovia, Adamsburg, or Jacksonville?

Answers

5. Infamy   6. True   **7. Four** (Ken's answer: three)   8. Monrovia

Can You Beat Ken?

Round 71

Questions

1. In a speech delivered September 11, 1998, President Bill Clinton admitted: "I don't think there is a fancy way to say that I have _____."

2. True or false? The Falkland Islands, which are 300 miles east of Argentina, are part of the United States.

3. Which five-star general was fired by President Truman: Douglas MacArthur, George Patton or Dwight Eisenhower?

4. What three fruits are on the Fruit of the Loom logo?

Answers

1. Sinned (Ken's answer: syphilis)   2. False (They are part of the United Kingdom.)
3. Douglas MacArthur   **4. Apple, grapes and gooseberries** (Ken's answer: apple, grapes and banana)

Can You Beat Ken?

Ken's score: 6

5. In "Happy Together," The Turtles sing: "Me and you and you and me,/ No matter how they toss the ____, it has to be."

6. True or false? Oil-rich Brunei shares the island of Borneo with Malaysia and Indonesia.

7. A deficiency in what vitamin will cause scurvy: vitamin D, vitamin C or vitamin E?

8. What was Mary Shelley's first novel, written when she was only 19 years old?

Answers

5. Dice   6. True   7. Vitamin C   8. *Frankenstein*

Can You Beat Ken?

Round 72

Questions

1. British Prime Minister Winston Churchill once described Russia as "a riddle wrapped in a mystery inside an _____."

2. True or false? E.B. White wrote *Charlotte's Web*, but most writers know him for the non-fiction masterpiece, *The Secret Life of Plants*.

3. What poet co-founded the famed San Francisco bookstore City Lights in 1953: Jack Kerouac, Allen Ginsberg or Lawrence Ferlinghetti?

4. What comet will not be visible to earthlings again until 2061?

Answers

1. Enigma   2. False   (The non-fiction masterpiece is *The Elements of Style*.)
3. Lawrence Ferlinghetti   4. Halley's Comet

Can You Beat Ken?

Ken's score: 7

5. The tagline for the 1992 movie *Wayne's World* promises: "You'll laugh. You'll cry. You'll ____."

6. True or false? The idea that the ends justify the means is a primary concept in Machiavelli's *The Prince*.

7. Who was the original host of *Wheel of Fortune*: Chuck Woolery, Wink Martindale or Pat Sajak?

8. What name is given to the time period during which Pablo Picasso's work mirrored his poverty?

Answers

5. Hurl (Ken's answer: spew)   6. True   7. Chuck Woolery   8. The Blue Period

Can You Beat Ken?

Round 73

Questions

1. According to the Book of Hebrews in the *Bible*, "Do not forget to entertain strangers, for by so doing some have unwittingly entertained _____."

2. True or false? The $100,000 bill features a portrait of Woodrow Wilson.

3. Who is the only male tennis player to win two Grand Slams: Pete Sampras, Bjorn Borg or Rod Laver?

4. What comedian coined the phrase "The devil made me do it."

Answers

1. Angels [Hebrews 13:2]   **2. True**   3. Rod Laver   4. Flip Wilson

Can You Beat Ken?

Ken's score: 6

5. The first line of Lincoln's Gettysburg Address is, "Four score and seven years ago our fathers brought forth, upon this continent, a new nation, conceived in _____ ... "

6. True or false? An artist must sell 1,000,000 CDs for the album to go platinum.

7. Which of these players does not belong on the list of top five lifetime base-stealers: Lou Brock, Ty Cobb or Barry Bonds?

8. Carole King broke out on her own in 1971 with what album?

Answers
5. Liberty   **6. True**   7. Barry Bonds   8. *Tapestry*

Can You Beat Ken?

Round 74

Questions

1. In her hit "Erotica," Madonna sings, "I'll be your mistress tonight/I'd like to put you in a ____."

2. True or false? If you left Luxembourg and headed south, the first sea you would reach would be the Black Sea.

3. South America lies completely below what important line of latitude: Tropic of Cancer, Equator or Prime Meridian?

4. Who wrote the 1971 hit song "American Pie"?

Answers

1. Trance (Ken's answer: headlock)   2. False (You would reach the Mediterranean Sea.)
3. Tropic of Cancer   4. Don McLean

Can You Beat Ken?

Ken's score: 5

5. John F. Kennedy began his inaugural speech with: " ... we observe today not a victory of party, but a celebration of _____ ... "

6. True or false? You could climb the Alps without leaving Italy.

7. Where did the largest earthquake recorded in the United States (magnitude 9.2) strike: Prince William Sound, AK; San Francisco, CA or New Madrid, MO?

8. In Three Dog Night's "Joy to the World," what was Jeremiah?

Answers

5. Freedom (Ken's answer: democracy)   6. True
7. Prince William Sound, AK (Ken's answer: New Madrid, MO)   8. A bullfrog

Can You Beat Ken?

Round 75

Questions

1. David Byrne of the Talking Heads sang "Psycho Killer," warning, "We are vain and we are blind/I hate people when they're not ____."

2. True or false? Constantinople was founded by Constantine the Great in 330 A.D. and is now called Istanbul.

3. Who was the Supreme Allied Commander during the campaign that liberated Europe in WWII: Dwight Eisenhower, William Westmoreland or George S. Patton?

4. In what city was Marco Polo born?

Answers

1. Polite (Ken's answer: mine)   2. True   3. Dwight Eisenhower   4. Venice, Italy

Can You Beat Ken?

Ken's score: 6

5. In his Sept. 11, 2001 address to the nation, President George W. Bush said, "These acts shattered steel, but they cannot dent the steel of American ____."

6. True or false? If you were traveling from the island of Majorca to Monte Carlo, you would have to cross the Mediterranean Sea.

7. Which Chief Justice of the Supreme Court handed down the decision to integrate American schools: Warren Burger, Louis Brandeis or Earl Warren?

8. What physical trait do champion athletes Babe Ruth, Steve Young, Martina Navratilova and Pelé all have in common?

Answers
5. Resolve (Ken's answer: pride)   6. True   7. Earl Warren   8. They are all left-handed.

Can You Beat Ken?

Round 76

Questions

1. The hit song from the soundtrack of Kevin Bacon's 1980s dance flick *Footloose* is titled "Let's Hear It For The _____."

2. True or false? French admiral Pierre-Charles Villeneuve stabbed himself through the heart after losing the Battle of Trafalgar.

3. Which state contains Camp David, called "Shangri-La" until Dwight Eisenhower renamed it: Maryland, Virginia or West Virginia?

4. What sport is physical education instructor Dr. James Naismith credited with developing?

Answers

1. Boy   **2. True**   3. Maryland   4. Basketball

Can You Beat Ken?

Ken's score: 6

5. DC Comics superhero Hal Jordan's alter ego is The _____ _____.

6. True or false? Shortstop phenom Nomar Garciaparra's real first name is Anthony.

7. What language is most commonly spoken in Greenland: Danish, Norwegian or English?

8. What medal was the U.S. awarded in Olympic basketball in 1972 after a controversial last second shot ended the game?

Answers
5. Green Lantern **6. True** 7. Danish 8. Silver (The USSR won gold.)

Can You Beat Ken?

Round 77

Questions

1. B.J. _____ recorded "Raindrops Keep Falling On My Head" – featured in the movie *Butch Cassidy and the Sundance Kid*.

2. True or false? Florida is the southernmost U.S. state.

3. Barbara Streisand won her first Oscar® for which film: *Funny Girl*, *Yentl* or *Hello Dolly*?

4. Who were the first father and son to play baseball in the major leagues at the same time?

Answers
1. Thomas   2. False (Hawaii is.)   3. *Funny Girl*
4. Ken Griffey, Sr. and Ken Griffey, Jr.

Can You Beat Ken?

Ken's score: 7

5. The city of Sarajevo is located in the country of Bosnia and _____.

6. True or false? Annie Oakley, born in 1860, was known as the nation's finest markswoman.

7. Where did carrots originate: The Netherlands, Brazil or Afghanistan?

8. Football fans flipped when this team finished with a perfect season in 1972 (17-0). Name the team.

Answers

5. Herzegovina   6. True   **7. Afghanistan** (Ken's answer: The Netherlands)   8. Miami Dolphins

Can You Beat Ken?

Round 78

Questions

1. Martin Scorsese documented the final performance of The Band in a movie called *The Last* _____.

2. True or false? The French and Indian Wars were fought on American soil from 1756 to 1763.

3. Which U.S. state is home to the largest population of Native Americans: California, Arizona or Nebraska?

4. Casey Martin won a court case against the PGA Tour, allowing him to use what tool in tournaments?

Answers

1. *Waltz*   2. True   **3. California** (Ken's answer: Arizona)   4. A golf cart

Can You Beat Ken?

Ken's score: 6

5. The name of Kate Hudson's character in *Almost Famous* is _____ _____.

6. True or false? W.E.B. DuBois was one of the founding members of the NAACP.

7. Which baseball player played the most games (3,308) for just one team: Lou Gehrig, Carl Yastrzemski or Cal Ripken, Jr.?

8. What California town served as the setting for Alfred Hitchcock's *The Birds*?

Answers

5. Penny Lane   6. True   **7. Carl Yastrzemski** (Ken's answer: Lou Gehrig)   8. Bodega Bay

Can You Beat Ken?

Round 79

Questions

1. The nickname for Kansas is the _____ State.

2. True or false? Sam Houston was born in Texas.

3. What part of the human body does bulbar polio attack: the spinal cord, the legs or the brain stem?

4. Doug Flutie's famous "Hail Mary" pass was thrown against what losing college team?

Answers

1. Sunflower   2. False (He was born in Virginia.)
3. The brain stem (Ken's answer: the legs)   4. The Miami Hurricanes

Can You Beat Ken?

Ken's score: 7

5. Woody Guthrie inspired a generation of folk singers with his song, "This ____ Is Your ____."

6. True or false? The Yukon River flows into the Bering Sea.

7. What actor, born Archibald Leach, played Archibald Cutter in the 1939 film *Gunga Din*: Cary Grant, David Niven or Burt Lancaster?

8. Which *Toy Story* character did Don Rickles provide the voice for?

Answers
5. Land, Land   6. True   7. Cary Grant   8. Mr. Potato Head

Can You Beat Ken?

Round 80

Questions

1. According to Rastafarian beliefs, the true Zion is located in _____.

2. True or false? The first completion of the Northwest Passage by water was carried out by Vitus Bering.

3. Which of Shakespeare's kings utters the famous line, "A horse! A horse! My kingdom for a horse!": Richard III, Henry V or King Lear?

4. Which of the screenwriters responsible for Mel Brooks' *High Anxiety* went on to direct *The Natural*?

Answers

1. Ethiopia   **2. False** (It was carried out by Roald Amundsen.)   3. King Richard III
4. Barry Levinson (Ken's answer: Jonathan Demme)

Can You Beat Ken?

Ken's score: 5

5. According to Groucho Marx: "The secret of life is honesty and fair dealing. If you can ____ that, you've got it made."

6. True or false? Hawaiian waterman legend Duke Kahanamoku won three Olympic gold medals over a 12-year span before finishing second at the age of 34 to a much younger Johnny Weismuller.

7. Which sea touches both Saudi Arabia and Ethiopia: Arabian Sea, Red Sea or Black Sea?

8. What planet is sometimes farther from the Sun than Pluto?

Answers

5. Fake (Ken's answer: overcome)   6. True   7. Red Sea   8. Neptune

Can You Beat Ken?

Round 81

Questions

1. According to the philosopher Eric Hoffer, "When people are free to do as they please, they usually _____ each other."

2. True or false? Besides playing Buck Rogers and Flash Gordon, sci-fi actor Buster Crabbe won an Olympic gold medal for swimming the 400-meter freestyle in 1932.

3. The king of Lydia in Asia Minor was the first to mint gold coins in the 6th century. What was his name: Midas, Croesus or Telemachus?

4. Which type of electrical current moves in only one direction?

Answers

1. Imitate (Ken's answer: hurt)   2. True   3. Croesus   4. DC (direct current)

Can You Beat Ken?

Ken's score: 6

5. According to Mark Twain, "Whenever you find you are on the side of the _____, it is time to pause and reflect."

6. True or false? The record for wins in the grueling Iditarod Trail sled dog race is four, held by Susan Butcher, from 1986 through 1988 and in 1990.

7. What did the U.S. Fugitive Slave Act of 1850 require be done with a runaway slave: be returned to owner, be set free or be put to death?

8. Which chemical element, whose symbol is the letter C, can be used to determine an object's age?

Answers

5. Majority   **6. True**   7. Be returned to owner   8. Carbon

Can You Beat Ken?

Round 82

Questions

1. According to Voltaire, "The secret of being _____ is to tell everything."

2. True or false? Boxing's first $1 million gate came with a bout between Frenchman Georges Carpentier and Jack Dempsey on July 2, 1921 in Jersey City, NJ.

3. What U.S. state was the first to allow women to vote: Wyoming, New Jersey or Georgia?

4. In 1923, Robert Millikan won a Nobel Prize for measuring the electrical charge of which atomic particle?

Answers
1. Tiresome (Ken's answer: trusted)   2. True   3. Wyoming   4. Electron

Can You Beat Ken?

Ken's score: 6

5. According to poet Robert Frost, "A jury consists of twelve people who determine which client has the better _____."

6. True or false? The first Olympic gold medal for beach volleyball was given to Misty May and Kerri Walsh in 2004.

7. Which U.S. president was responsible for the Louisiana Purchase, which doubled the size of the U.S.: George Washington, Thomas Jefferson or Millard Fillmore?

8. Ursa Major contains seven stars that form a pattern particularly appropriate for the Milky Way. What is this formation known as?

Answers

5. Lawyer   **6. False** (It was given to Kent Steffes and Karch Kiraly in 1996.)
7. Thomas Jefferson   8. The Big Dipper

Can You Beat Ken?

Round 83

Questions

1. According to Walt Disney, "It's kind of ____ to do the impossible."

2. True or false? Jane Seymour played Contessa Teresa "Tracy" Di Vicenzo Bond, the only woman James Bond married.

3. How much was the British tax levied on every pound of tea that caused the Boston Tea Party: one English pound, two cents or three pence?

4. What book by Dr. Alex Comfort was subtitled "A Gourmet Guide to Lovemaking"?

Answers

1. Fun   2. False (The part was played by Diana Rigg in *On Her Majesty's Secret Service*.)
3. Three pence (Ken's answer: two cents)   4. *The Joy of Sex*

Can You Beat Ken?

Ken's score: 6

5. *A Tale of Two Cities* by Charles Dickens opens with, "It was the best of times, it was the worst of times, it was the age of _____ ... "

6. True or false? The only two continents located completely in the Southern Hemisphere are Australia and Antarctica.

7. Which amendment to the U.S. Constitution brought in prohibition: the Tenth, the Thirteenth or the Eighteenth?

8. N.C., Andrew and Henriette are all members of what famous and highly successful family of painters?

Answers
5. Wisdom (Ken's answer: happiness)   6. True   7. The Eighteenth   8. Wyeth

Can You Beat Ken?

Round 84

Questions

1. James Joyce's *A Portrait of the Artist as a Young Man* begins with, "Once upon a time and a very good time it was there was a _____ coming down along the road ... "

2. True or false? The population of India is mostly Buddhist.

3. When was the copper penny first minted by the United States: 1792, 1811 or 1910?

4. When Sir Francis Drake landed in what is now California, he dedicated the land to Queen Elizabeth and called it what: San Francisco, New Albion or Macaroni?

Answers

1. Moocow   2. False (Hindu)   **3. 1792** (Ken's answer: 1910)
4. **New Albion** (Ken's answer: Macaroni)

Can You Beat Ken?

Ken's score: 6

5. Carson McCullers' *The Heart is a Lonely Hunter* begins with, "In the town there were two _____, and they were always together."

6. True or false? The population of Northern Ireland is mostly Catholic.

7. On his first American tour, who did Jimi Hendrix open for: The Yardbirds, The Monkees or Pink Floyd?

8. Name one of Marshall Mathers' alter egos.

Answers
5. Mutes   6. False (It is mostly Protestant.)   7. The Monkees   8. Slim Shady or Eminem

Can You Beat Ken?

Round 85

Questions

1. Rita Mae Brown's *Rubyfruit Jungle* begins with: "No one remembers her
_____."

2. True or false? In Rome and the rest of Italy, nearly 100% of the residents
are Catholic.

3. What is a sacher torte: a cake, a dance step or a geometric shape?

4. What branch of Jewish Orthodox mysticism does Madonna study?

Answers
1. Beginnings (Ken's answer: name)   2. True   3. A cake   4. Kabbalah

Can You Beat Ken?

Ken's score: 6

5. F. Scott Fitzgerald's *The Great Gatsby* begins with, "In my younger and more _____ years my father gave me some advice ... "

6. True or false? John Wayne's real name was Marion Morrison.

7. What kind of animal is Dolly, who became famous in 1997 for her cloned genes: cat, sheep or mouse?

8. What does the "M" in "CD-ROM" stand for?

Answers
5. Vulnerable (Ken's answer: carefree)   6. True   7. Sheep   8. Memory

Can You Beat Ken?

Round 86

Questions

1. William Faulkner's *The Sound and the Fury* begins with, "Through the fence, between the curling flower spaces, I could see them _____."

2. True or false? Handbag designer Kate Spade is sister-in-law of comedian David Spade.

3. Who is the only major league pitcher to have 100 saves and 100 complete games: Eric Gagne, Dave Righetti or Dennis Eckersley?

4. On the Periodic Table, what element is mysteriously abbreviated as Hg?

Answers

1. Hitting (Ken's answer: fighting)   2. True   3. Dennis Eckersley   4. Mercury

Can You Beat Ken?

Ken's score: 7

5. When the Supremes performed "Stop! In the Name of Love," Diana Ross sang, "I've tried so hard, hard to be patient/Hoping you'd stop this _____ ... "

6. True or false? The family dog on *The Jetsons* is named Cosmo.

7. One of the greatest works of social protest, Picasso's *Guernica*, depicts the horrors of what war: the Spanish Civil War, World War I or World War II?

8. What faith do John Travolta, Kirstie Alley and Tom Cruise all adhere to?

Answers

5. Infatuation   6. False (His name is Astro.)
7. Spanish Civil War   8. Scientology

Can You Beat Ken?

Round 87

Questions

1. William Golding's *Lord of the Flies* begins with: "The boy with fair hair lowered himself down the last few feet of rock and began to pick his way towards the _____."

2. True or false? *USA Today* sells more copies each day than any other daily in the U.S.

3. Which of Kurt Vonnegut Jr.'s novels takes place in Dresden and outer space: *Cat's Cradle*, *Slaughterhouse-Five* or *Mother Night*?

4. What kind of rock is formed from volcanic action or intense heat?

Answers

1. Lagoon (Ken's answer: beach)   2. True   3. *Slaughterhouse-Five*   4. Igneous

Can You Beat Ken?

Ken's score: 7

5. Elvis Presley opens "Jailhouse Rock" with , "The ____ threw a party in the county jail./The prison band was there and they began to wail."

6. True or false? Sigourney Weaver made her movie debut with a very small part in *Annie Hall*.

7. Which artist was not one of the three great names of the High Renaissance: Michelangelo, Raphael or Rossetti?

8. What letter does not appear on the Periodic Table?

Answers
5. Warden   6. True   7. Rossetti   8. J

Can You Beat Ken?

Round 88

Questions

1. Alice Walker's *The Color Purple* begins with, "You better not never tell nobody but ___."

2. True or false? Tennessee Williams was born in Mississippi.

3. What idiotic character did Steve Martin play in *The Jerk*: Navin R. Johnson, Oliver Klozoff or George Stanley Banks?

4. In 1982, Michael Jordan led which southern school to the NCAA basketball title?

Answers

1. God   2. True   **3. Navin R. Johnson** (Ken's answer: Oliver Klozoff)   4. North Carolina

Can You Beat Ken?

Ken's score: 5

5. The first verse of the Grateful Dead's "Casey Jones" includes the lyrics, "Trouble ahead, trouble behind,/And you know that _____ just crossed my mind."

6. True or false? A fairy named Puck can be found in Shakespeare's *The Taming of the Shrew*.

7. Who played Al Pacino's "wife" in *Dog Day Afternoon*: Chris Sarandon, Susan Sarandon or John Cazale?

8. In 1994, what divisions were added to baseball's National and American Leagues?

Answers

5. Notion (Ken's answer: death)   6. False (He's in *A Midsummer Night's Dream*.)
7. Chris Sarandon (Ken's answer: John Cazale)   8. Central Divisions

Can You Beat Ken?

Round 89

Questions

1. Agatha Christie began her famous whodunit *The Mirror Crack'd* with, "Miss Jane _____ was sitting by her window."

2. True or false? John Knowles' novel *A Separate Peace* takes place during World War I.

3. Who played Denzel Washington's father in his 1981 movie debut *Carbon Copy*: George Segal, Jack Lemmon or Sidney Poitier?

4. David Robinson of the San Antonio Spurs graduated from the U.S. Naval Academy. What rank provides his nickname?

Answers
1. Marple   2. False (It takes place during World War II.)
3. George Segal (Ken's answer: Jack Lemmon)   4. Admiral

Can You Beat Ken?

Ken's score: 6

5. Michael Ondaatje began *The English Patient* with, "She stands up in the _____ where she has been working and looks into the distance."

6. True or false? Franklin D. Roosevelt wrote *Profiles in Courage* while recuperating from back surgery.

7. Flickertail, North Dakota is named for what type of animal: squirrel, bird or snake?

8. What rock group performs the opening music for all three *CSI* TV series?

Answers

5. Garden   6. False (John F. Kennedy wrote it.)
7. Squirrel (Ken's answer: bird)   8. The Who

Can You Beat Ken?

Round 90

Questions

1. What famous gun fighter and poker player was also a dentist and died of tuberculosis at the age of thirty-five?

2. True or false? Irving Berlin wrote the song "God Bless America," yet he was born in Russia.

3. What is the longest mountain range on Earth: the Himalayas, the Rockies or the Mid-Ocean Range ?

4. What is the nickname for the 45-caliber machine gun?

Answers
1. "Doc" Holliday   2. True   **3. The Mid-Ocean Range** (Ken's answer: Rockies)
4. Tommy gun

Can You Beat Ken?

Ken's score: 6

5. Robert Heinlein's sci-fi classic, *Stranger in a Strange Land*, opens with, "Once upon a time there was a _____ named Valentine Michael Smith."

6. True or false? Leonardo da Vinci's *The Last Supper* is the world's most expensive painting.

7. What is the first major mountain range west of Washington D.C.: Adirondack Mountains, Ozark Mountains or Appalachian Mountains?

8. Professional golfer Jack Nicklaus won more major championships (18) than any other player. What's his nickname?

Answers

5. Martian   6. False (*Mona Lisa* is estimated at $100 million.)
7. Appalachian Mountains (Ken's answer: Ozarks)   8. The Golden Bear

Can You Beat Ken?

Round 91

Questions

1. Isaac Asimov's *I, Robot* begins with, "I looked at my _____ and I didn't like them."

2. True or false? The Tony Awards® are named after Antoinette Perry.

3. Who hit #1 in 1964 with the song "Oh, Pretty Woman:" Roy Orbison, Del Shannon or Smokey Robinson?

4. In Euros or U.S. dollars, what is the winner's purse of the Ryder Cup matches that pit the best American golfers against the best of Europe?

Answers
1. Notes (Ken's answer: odds)   2. True   3. Roy Orbison
4. Zero (Ken's answer: $2 million)

Can You Beat Ken?

Ken's score: 5

5. Mark Twain's classic *Tom Sawyer* begins with, " '____!' "

6. True or false? The harpsichord was invented before the piano.

7. Which Disney film was the first full-length animated feature ever to be nominated for a Best Picture Oscar®: *Fantasia*, *The Lion King* or *Beauty and the Beast*?

8. Which state touches both the Ohio and the Potomac Rivers?

Answers
5. Tom   6. True   7. *Beauty and the Beast*   **8. West Virginia** (Ken's answer: Virginia)

Can You Beat Ken?

Round 92

Questions

1. Ray Bradbury's futuristic novel, *Fahrenheit 451*, begins with: "It was a pleasure to _____."

2. True or false? Every year, the President of the United States presents the National Medal of Arts awarded by the National Endowment for the Arts.

3. Which boy band member made a solo album that included the hit "Cry Me a River": Nick Lachey, Nick Carter or Justin Timberlake?

4. In which body of water is the Isle of Youth located?

Answers
1. Burn   2. True   3. Justin Timberlake
4. The Caribbean Sea (Ken's answer: the English Channel)

Can You Beat Ken?

Ken's score: 5

5. The tagline for the 1978 frat party hit *Animal House* declares: "Animal House is an _____ film."

6. True or false? *Bury My Heart At Wounded Knee* was written by Russell Means.

7. As of 2005, Meryl Streep has been nominated for 13 Academy Awards®. How many has she won: one, two or five?

8. The lowest point in South America is in what country?

Answers
5. Educational (Ken's answer: appalling)   6. False (It was written by Dee Brown.)
7. Two   **8. Argentina** (Ken's answer: Brazil)

Can You Beat Ken?

Round 93

Questions

1. At the beginning of "Born to Run," Bruce Springsteen sings, "In the day we sweat it out in the streets of a _____ American dream."

2. True or false? In a poem by Eugene Field, the Calico Cat got into a tussle with the Gingham Dog.

3. Which U.S. state receives the most lightning strikes per year: Florida, California or Texas?

4. What did pitcher Bob Feller do on April 16, 1940, for the first and only time in baseball history?

Answers
1. Runaway   2. True   **3. Florida** (Ken's answer: Texas)
4. Pitch a no-hitter at a season opener. (Ken's answer: Lose a no-hitter.)

Can You Beat Ken?

Ken's score: 5

5. Albert Camus' existentialist classic, *The Stranger*, begins with these three words, "_____ died today."

6. True or false? Every year, the Centers for Disease Control report about 10,000 cases of "necrotizing fasciitis," or flesh-eating disease.

7. What 565-mile-long river forms the northern border between Germany and Poland: the Oder, Loire or Ganges?

8. What popular spectator sport has featured Mr. October, the Georgia Peach and the Iron Horse?

Answers

5. Mother   **6. False** (They report approximately 600 cases per year.)
7. Oder   8. Baseball

Can You Beat Ken?

Round 94

Questions

1. The Moody Blues began their hit song, "Nights in White Satin" with, "Nights in white satin,/Never reaching the ___ ... "

2. True or false? When jump-starting a dead car battery, connect the positive pole of the dead battery to the assist battery first, then the negative pole of the assist battery to the dead car's engine block.

3. What two countries border Andorra: Spain and France, Germany and Austria or Algeria and Morocco?

4. In what Alaskan city does the world famous Iditarod Trail dog sled race finish?

Answers

1. End (Ken's answer: dawn)   2. True   3. Spain and France   4. Nome

Can You Beat Ken?

Ken's score: 6

5. The chorus to Jessica Simpson's "Irresistible" ends with, "His ways are ____, /irresistible to me."

6. True or false? The Impressionist masterpiece titled "I and the Village" was painted by Claude Monet.

7. What is Cuba's official language: Spanish, Cuban or Castilian?

8. What pro quarterback made a cameo appearance in the film *There's Something About Mary*?

Answers
5. Powerful (Ken's answer: mysterious)   6. False (Marc Chagall painted it.)
7. Spanish   8. Brett Favre

Can You Beat Ken?

Round 95

Questions

1. The Dixie Chicks' first hit, "I Can Love You Better" begins with, "She's got you wrapped up in her _____ and lace./Tied around her little finger."

2. True or false? Stephen King made his writing debut with the novel *Carrie*.

3. Tasmania is an island south of what continent: South America, Australia or Africa?

4. The San Francisco 49ers retired what quarterback's number in 1997?

Answers

1. Satin (Ken's answer: ribbons)   2. True   3. Australia   4. Joe Montana's #16

Can You Beat Ken?

Ken's score: 5

5. Nobel Prize winner Pearl Buck began *The Good Earth* with: "It was Wang Lung's _____ day."

6. True or false? When Oliver Stone attended NYU, Martin Scorsese was his professor.

7. Which U.S. city has the largest area: Anchorage, Los Angeles or New York?

8. The film *Brian's Song* is based on the true story of Brian Piccolo, who played for what pro football team?

Answers
5. Marriage (Ken's answer: wedding) **6. True** 7. Anchorage 8. The Chicago Bears

Can You Beat Ken?

Round 96

Questions

1. Bill Clinton's favorite Fleetwood Mac song, "Don't Stop" includes the lines, "Why not think about _____ to come,/And not about the things that you've done ... "

2. True or false? Scoville units, named after pharmacisct Wilbur Scoville, are the units of measure used to rate the heat of peppers.

3. Which state takes its name from the Yuchi Indian word for "meeting place": Nebraska, Minnesota or Tennessee?

4. In what state did the American Civil War end with General Robert E. Lee's surrender at the Appomattox Courthouse?

Answers
1. Times (Ken's answer: tomorrow)   2. True   3. Tennessee   4. Virginia

Can You Beat Ken?

Ken's score: 6

5. Nobel Prize winner Saul Bellow begins *Humboldt's Gift* with, "The book of _____ published by Von Humboldt Fleisher in the Thirties was an immediate hit."

6. True or false? Orson Welles' *Citizen Kane* is believed to be loosely based on the life of publishing magnate William Randolph Hearst.

7. The Columbia River touches what two states: Oklahoma and Texas, Idaho and Montana or Oregon and Washington?

8. What British admiral is credited with winning the Battle of Trafalgar?

Answers
5. Ballads (Ken's answer: poetry)   6. True
7. Oregon and Washington   8. Horatio Nelson

Can You Beat Ken?

Round 97

Questions

1. Justin Timberlake's first solo hit, "Like I Love You," contains the chorus, "Maybe we'll ____ tonight/I just wanna love you, baby."

2. True or false? Cleveland is the home of Motown Records' original recording studio.

3. In which U.S. state would you visit the Hopi reservation: New Mexico, Virginia or Arizona?

4. The invasion by Iraq in 1990 of what country touched off the U.S. military operations known as Desert Shield and eventually Desert Storm?

Answers
1. Fly (Ken's answer: dance)   2. False (It's original home is Detroit.)
3. Arizona   4. Kuwait

Can You Beat Ken?

Ken's score: 6

5. In the first verse of "Money," Pink Floyd sings, "Money, it's a gas. Grab that cash with both hands and make a _____."

6. True or false? The *Godfather, Part II* is the only sequel to win Best Picture at the Academy Awards®.

7. In which U.S. state is the city of Truth or Consequences located: New Mexico, South Dakota or Nebraska?

8. In 2005, who was the leader of North Korea?

Answers

5. Stash (Ken's answer: splash)   6. False (*The Lord of the Rings: The Return of the King* won in 2003.)
7. New Mexico   8. Kim Jong-Il

Can You Beat Ken?

Round 98

Questions

1. Avril Lavigne opens "Sk8ter Boi" with the lyrics, "He was a boy,/She was a girl,/Can I make it any more _____."

2. True or false? Zsa Zsa Gabor co-starred with Eddie Albert in the 1960s TV hit *Green Acres*.

3. What city is New Hampshire's only seaport and the site of its first settlement: Concord, Portsmouth or Newport?

4. What country has the smallest landmass –.17 square miles?

Answers

1. Obvious (Ken's answer: clear)   2. False (Her sister Eva did.)
3. Portsmouth   4. Vatican City

Can You Beat Ken?

Ken's score: 6

5. Nat King Cole's "Mona Lisa" begins with, "Mona Lisa, Mona Lisa, men have named you/You're so like the lady with the _____ smile."

6. True or false? The first TV remote control developed in 1950 was called The Lazy Bones.

7. What is the panda's native country: Bangladesh, China or Australia?

8. Who was the first vice president to ascend to the presidency of the U.S. after a president resigned?

Answers
5. Mystic (Ken's answer: famous)   6. True   7. China   8. Gerald Ford

Can You Beat Ken?

Round 99

Questions

1. The Beatles begin "Across The Universe" with the lyric, "_____ are flowing out like endless rain into a paper cup."

2. True or false? "Video Killed the Radio Star" by the Buggles was the first video shown on MTV when the network launched in 1981.

3. How far does electricity move in a wire every nanosecond: one inch, one foot or one yard?

4. What was John F. Kennedy's wife's maiden name?

Answers
1. Words   2. True   **3. One foot** (Ken's answer: one yard)
4. Jacqueline Lee Bouvier

Can You Beat Ken?

Ken's score: 6

5. Joni Mitchell's song, "The Circle Game" begins with the lyric, "Yesterday a child came out to wonder/Caught a _____ inside a jar."

6. True or false? In the children's book series, Captain Underpants's secret weakness is spray starch.

7. At 726 feet in height, the Hoover Dam controls the flow of what: the Colorado, Gila or Platte River?

8. What is the address of the White House?

Answers
5. Dragonfly (Ken's answer: frog)   6. True   7. Colorado River
8. 1600 Pennsylvania Ave., Washington, D.C.

Can You Beat Ken?

Round 100

Questions

1. In "Moondance," Van Morrison sings, "A _____ night to make romance/ 'neath the cover of October skies."

2. True or false? The dress Marilyn Monroe wore in *The Seven Year Itch* that flew up over the subway grating is owned by Elton John.

3. Which U.S. state holds the record for the highest temperature: Texas, California or Arizona?

4. Who was the first U.S. president to ride in an automobile and the first to travel outside the country (to Panama)?

Answers
1. Fantabulous   **2. False** (Debbie Reynolds owns it.)
3. California   4. Theodore Roosevelt

Can You Beat Ken?

Ken's score: 6

5. "All Along the Watchtower" by Bob Dylan begins, "There must be some kind of way out of here/Said the _____ to the thief."

6. True or false? The mascot featured in Cheetos® ads with the tagline, "It's not easy being cheesy®," is Chester Cheetah.

7. What is deoxyribonucleic acid better known as: NutraSweet®, nerve gas or DNA?

8. Who threw out the first pitch of Game Three at the 2001 World Series, held at Yankee Stadium?

Answers
5. Joker   6. True   7. DNA
8. President George W. Bush (Ken's answer: Rudy Giuliani)

Can You Beat Ken?

Round 101

Questions

1. Kurt Cobain lists four things in Nirvana's song "Smells Like Teen Spirit," "A mulatto/An albino/A mosquito/My _____ ... "

2. True or false? In Denmark, one says "Skol" to make a toast.

3. Which man oversaw construction of the Panama Canal: G. Washington de Lessep, G. Washington Goethals or G. Washington Carver?

4. Who is Paris Hilton's co-star on the TV series *The Simple Life*?

Answers

1. Libido   2. True   **3. G. Washington Goethals** (Ken's answer: G. Washington de Lessep)
4. Nicole Richie

Can You Beat Ken?

Ken's score: 6

5. In the chorus of "Hotel California," the Eagles sing, "Welcome to the Hotel California/Such a _____ place ... "

6. True or false? California is the U.S. state with the longest coastline.

7. Who was president when the SALT agreement was signed: Lyndon B. Johnson, John F. Kennedy or Richard Nixon?

8. What was the name of the New York loft that was home base for Andy Warhol and his Pop art entourage?

Answers

5. Lovely   6. False (Alaska has the longest coastline.)   7. Richard Nixon
8. The Factory (Ken's answer: The Studio)

Can You Beat Ken?

Round 102

Questions

1. The Billie Holiday song "Strange Fruit" begins, "Southern trees bear strange fruit,/ _____ on the leaves, ____ on the root."

2. True or false? Finland is home to the Geiranger and the Nord Fjords.

3. Richard Bachman, author of *The Regulars*, is a pen name for which author: Robert Ludlum, Stephen King or Dean Koontz?

4. What 1988 John Waters movie became a Broadway hit?

Answers
1. Blood...blood (Ken's answer: dust)   2. False (Norway is.)
3. Stephen King   4. *Hairspray*

Can You Beat Ken?

Ken's score: 6

5. Led Zeppelin's classic, "Stairway to Heaven" ends with the line: "And she's _____ a stairway to heaven."

6. True or false? The Nile River runs north from Lake Victoria to the Mediterranean Sea.

7. *One Flew Over the Cuckoo's Nest* won five Oscars®. For which category did it not win: Best Picture, or Best Actor or Best Editing?

8. Who was the last men's tennis champion to win at Wimbledon by defeating every opponent he faced without losing a single set?

Answers

5. Buying (Ken's answer: climbing) 6. True 7. Best Editing 8. Bjorn Borg

Can You Beat Ken?

Round 103

Questions

1. The last line of Cat Stevens's song "Peace Train" is, "Oh, peace train take this _____ ,/Come take me home again."

2. True or false? The Arabian Peninsula is the world's largest peninsula.

3. Which of these international writers has not won the Nobel Prize for Literature: Salman Rushdie, Pablo Neruda or Jean-Paul Sartre?

4. What is the hottest planet in the solar system?

Answers
1. Country   2. True   3. Salman Rushdie   **4. Venus** (Ken's answer: Mercury)

Can You Beat Ken?

Ken's score: 7

5. Bob Dylan's masterpiece, "Blowin' in the Wind" begins with, "How many _____ must a man walk down/Before you call him a man?"

6. True or false? The role of Tiny in the 1992 comedy *Wayne's World* is played by rock legend Meat Loaf.

7. Which African country is closest to the Equator: Zambia, Mozambique or Kenya?

8. The flag of which South American country features a sun with a face on it, placed in the upper left corner?

Answers
5. Roads   6. True   7. Kenya   8. Uruguay

Can You Beat Ken?

Round 104

Questions

1. The final verse of the song Frank Sinatra made famous, "My Way," begins with, "For what is a man, what has he got?/If not _____, then he has naught."

2. True or false? Monaco's population is around 30,000 people.

3. What famously beautiful Egyptian queen was the wife of Akhenaton: Cleopatra, Ankh Su Namun or Nefertiti?

4. Who said, "Blessed are the meek for they shall inherit the earth?"

Answers
1. Himself (Ken's answer: pride)   2. True   3. Nefertiti   4. Jesus [Matthew 5:5]

Can You Beat Ken?

Ken's score: 6

5. Franklin D. Roosevelt said, "This generation of Americans has a rendezvous with _____."

6. True or false? Vesuvius is the largest volcano in the world.

7. Who painted "Boy with a Pipe," the highest-priced painting ever to be sold at auction: Rembrandt, Picasso or Michelangelo?

8. Which continent has the greatest number of countries?

Answers

5. Destiny   6. False (Mauna Loa, HI is the largest.)
7. Picasso (Ken's answer: Michelangelo)   8. Africa

Can You Beat Ken?

Round 105

Questions

1. According to Aesop, "Familiarity breeds _____."

2. True or false? Ren of the TV cartoon *Ren and Stimpy* is a dog.

3. What is the name of the actress who rides on the handlebars in *Butch Cassidy and the Sundance Kid*: Ali McGraw, Katharine Ross or Julie Christie?

4. What is the name of Heather Graham's character in *Austin Powers: The Spy Who Shagged Me*?

Answers
1. Contempt   2. True   3. Katharine Ross   4. Felicity Shagwell

Can You Beat Ken?

Ken's score: 7

5. The 1987 Beastie Boys song called upon each person to "fight for your right to _____."

6. True or false? When California residential garbage was analyzed, the largest stream of inorganic waste (27%) came from paper that could have been recycled.

7. Who is Don Quixote's loyal squire: Florentino Ariza, Sancho Panza or La Mancha?

8. The book *Memoirs of a Geisha* chronicles the hard lives of young women living in what Japanese city?

Answers

5. Party   6. True   7. Sancho Panza   **8. Kyoto** (Ken's answer: Tokyo)

Can You Beat Ken?

Round 106

Questions

1. In the song "Blinded by the Light", Manfred Mann's Earth Band sings: "Mama always told me not to look into the eyes of the sun. But Mama, that's where the _____ is!"

2. True or false? The hippo's only known enemies are lions and tigers.

3. What is the 1969 book that starts with: "All this happened, more or less": *Slaughterhouse-Five*, *Catch-22* or *Portnoy's Complaint*?

4. What is the Greek word for romantic love?

Answers

1. Fun (Ken's answer: light)   2. False (other hippos and humans)
3. *Slaughterhouse-Five* (Ken's answer: *Portnoy's Complaint*)   4. Eros

Can You Beat Ken?

Ken's score: 5

5. In the 1970s hit, The Commodores sing, "Well _____ a brick house."

6. True or false? The closest to Richard Petty's record of 200 career NASCAR wins is Jeff Gordon with 58.

7. What statement does Dadaism make: don't follow any rules, respect your father or paint things backwards?

8. What mischievous fictional girl lives in the Plaza Hotel with her nanny and her turtle?

Answers
5. She's (Ken's answer: buy)   6. False (It's Dave Pearson with 105.)
7. Don't follow any rules.   8. Eloise

Can You Beat Ken?

Round 107

Questions

1. According to Benjamin Franklin, "Remember that time is _____.

2. True or false? Belgium hasn't been in a foreign war since 1515.

3. Who is credited with designing New York City's Central Park: Frederick Law Olmstead, Robert Moses or Cass Gilbert?

4. What poet wrote about the honeymoon of a bird and a feline in a "beautiful pea-green boat"?

Can You Beat Ken?

Ken's score: 6

5. In the original 1971 film *Willy Wonka & the Chocolate Factory*, Gene Wilder sings, "If you want to view _____, simply look around and view it. Anything you want to, do it. Want to change the world? There's nothing to it."

6. True or false? According to the Billiard Congress of America's official rules of 9-Ball, if a player inadvertently sinks the 9-ball while making a legal shot, then s/he automatically loses the game.

7. What medal is given for the most distinguished contribution to American children's literature: the Caldecott Medal, the Newbery Medal or the Edgar Award?

8. Name the author and Ph.D. best known for writing the book *Men Are from Mars, Women Are from Venus*.

Answers

5. Paradise   6. False (That player wins.)
7. The Newbery Medal (Ken's answer: The Caldecott Medal)   8. John Gray, Ph.D.

Can You Beat Ken?

Round 108

Questions

1. William Gibson's seminal cyberpunk novel *Neuromancer* opens with, "The sky above the port was the color of television, tuned to a ____ channel."

2. True or false? Pitching ace Pedro Martinez began his major league career with the Expos.

3. Which of these American writers has not won the Nobel Prize for Literature: John Steinbeck, Toni Morrison or Norman Mailer?

4. Who wrote *Presumed Innocent*, published in 1987?

Can You Beat Ken?

Ken's score: 5

5. Jim Croce's 1973 song describes Leroy Brown as "Badder than old King Kong, meaner than a _____ _____."

6. True or false? Oscar Wilde wrote in the play *The Matchmaker*, "Money is like manure, it's not worth a thing unless it's spread around ... "

7. Who is the only designated hitter to ever win the World Series MVP: Reggie Jackson, Jose Canseco or Paul Molitor?

8. What is the female portion of a flowering plant called?

Answers

5. Junkyard dog   6. False (Thornton Wilder wrote *The Matchmaker*.)
7. Paul Molitor (Ken's answer: Jose Canseco)   8. The pistil

Can You Beat Ken?

Round 109

Questions

1. *The World According to Garp* by John Irving begins with, "Garp's mother, Jenny Fields, was arrested in Boston in 1942 for _____ a man in a movie theater."

2. True or false? Sister Helen Prejean wrote the nonfiction book on which the 1996 movie *Dead Man Walking* was based.

3. Who wrote *A Room With a View*: E.M. Forster, D.H. Lawrence or L.M. Montgomery?

4. The temperature of a star's surface is determined by the rate at which hydrogen is being converted into what?

Answers

1. Wounding (Ken's answer: soliciting)   2. True   3. E.M. Forster   4. Helium

Can You Beat Ken?

Ken's score: 6

5. Larry McMurtry's novel *Terms of Endearment* begins with, " 'The success of a marriage invariably depends on the _____,' Mrs. Greenway said."

6. True or false? The Smucker's product that combines peanut butter and jelly in one jar is called Goober.

7. In what movie do Jeff Bridges and Beau Bridges actually play brothers: *The Big Lebowski, Thunderbolt and Lightfoot* or *The Fabulous Baker Boys*?

8. What is the common name for the phenomenon which causes masts and spires to appear to burn or glow?

Answers
5. Woman (Ken's answer: children)   6. True
7. *The Fabulous Baker Boys*   8. St. Elmo's Fire

Can You Beat Ken?

Round 110

Questions

1. Ian Fleming begins *Goldfinger* with, "James Bond, with two double _____ inside him, sat back in the final departure lounge of Miami Airport and thought about life and death."

2. True or false? Like Britney Spears and Christina Aguilera, Jessica Simpson appeared on *The Mickey Mouse Club*.

3. Which half of the 1980s hit-making duo Wham! went on to solo pop stardom: Daryl Hall, Boy George or George Michael?

4. What direction is 180 degrees from North on a compass?

Answers
1. Bourbons (Ken's answer: martinis)   2. False   3. George Michael   4. South

Can You Beat Ken?

Ken's score: 6

5. In "Crocodile Rock," Elton John waxes nostalgic with the words, "I remember when _____ was young, me and Suzie had so much fun."

6. True or false? Squidworth is SpongeBob's best friend.

7. Which is the only mammal unable to jump: the hippopotamus, elephant or sloth?

8. What nursery rhyme did Thomas Edison recite for the first phonographic recording?

Answers

5. Rock   6. False (Patrick is.)   **7. The elephant** (Ken's answer: the hippopotamus)
8. "Mary Had a Little Lamb"

Can You Beat Ken?

Round 111

Questions

1. The TV show *Cardsharks* opened with the teaser, "Ace is high, deuce is low. Call it right and win the_____."

2. True or false? The first athlete to compete in the same Olympic event four times was Al Oerter.

3. Who said: "This is the sort of English up with which I will not put": Oscar Wilde, George Bernard Shaw or Winston Churchill?

4. Who wrote *Lonesome Dove* and *The Last Picture Show*?

Answers
1. Dough   2. True (in the discus throw)
3. Winston Churchill (Ken's answer: George Bernard Shaw)   4. Larry McMurtry

Can You Beat Ken?

Ken's score: 6

5. After her escape from the foundering Titanic, Margaret Tobin Brown was given the nickname "The _____ Molly Brown."

6. True or false? Actor Jack Lemmon was born on an elevator.

7. *Soul Train*, one of the longest-running programs in the history of television, originated in 1971 in what U.S. city: Chicago, Detroit or Philadelphia?

8. The Indigo Girls sing about which Italian astromomer?

Answers

5. Unsinkable   6. True   **7. Chicago** (Ken's answer: Detroit)   8. Galileo Galilei

Can You Beat Ken?

Round 112

Questions

1. In 2002, Kate Bosworth starred as a surfer girl determined to rule at the Pipemaster's Invitational in the film *Blue* _____.

2. True or false? The state of Nevada is named for the Spanish word that means "snowcapped."

3. Who penned the inspirational children's story *The Little Engine that Could*: Roald Dahl, Watty Piper or Virginia Lee Burton?

4. What Missouri town shares its name with the first actor to play TV's Lone Ranger?

Answers

1. *Crush*   2. True   **3. Watty Piper** (Ken's answer: Virginia Lee Burton)   4. Clayton

Can You Beat Ken?

Ken's score: 5

5.   In her novel *Mansfield Park* Jane Austen wrote, "A large _____ is the best recipe for happiness I have ever heard of."

6.   True or false? Dr. Seuss's first book, published in 1937, was called *And to Think That I Saw It on Mulberry Street*.

7.   What animal has the best sense of hearing: the dolphin, skunk or elephant?

8.   In the 1978 movie *Superman*, what color underwear did Lois Lane wear while asking Superman about X-ray vision?

Answers
5. Income (Ken's answer: family)   6. True
7. The dolphin (Ken's answer: the elephant)   8. Pink

Can You Beat Ken?

Round 113

Questions

1. Eleanor Roosevelt once said, "No one can make you feel_____without your consent."

2. True or false? The 1993 film *Cool Runnings* is a story about the Jamaican Olympic bobsled team.

3. What college did Wilt Chamberlain attend: University of Kansas, University of Pennsylvania or University of Kentucky?

4. What Native American is credited with helping the pilgrims and served as a guide to Fernando Gorges?

Answers

1. Inferior   2. True   **3. Kansas** (Ken's answer: Kentucky)   4. Squanto

Can You Beat Ken?

Ken's score: 5

5.   Aristotle wrote that "Dignity consists not in possessing honors, but in the consciousness that we _____ them."

6.   True or false? The basic shape of a snowflake is a hexagon.

7.   For what ailment might an Egyptian doctor have told a patient to swallow a dead mouse: a sore throat, the common cold or indigestion?

8.   Who was Marilyn Monroe's famous acting teacher and mentor?

Answers
5. Deserve (Ken's answer: earned)   6. True
7. A sore throat (Ken's answer: the common cold)   8. Lee Strasberg

Can You Beat Ken?

Round 114

Questions

1. In Buddy Holly's song "Oh Boy", he sings with anticipation, "All of my life I've been a-waitin'. Tonight there'll be no_____."

2. True or false? Marlin Perkins was the original host of *Wild Kingdom*, which debuted in 1963.

3. What causes blond hair to turn green after a dip in the pool: shampoo in the gym, metals in the pool or chlorine?

4. What mythical beast serves as the symbol of the Boston Athletic Association, and appears on the medals awarded for the Boston Marathon?

Answers
1. Hesitatin'   2. True   **3. Metals in the pool** (Ken's answer: chlorine)
4. Unicorn (Ken's answer: Pegasus)

Can You Beat Ken?

Ken's score: 5

5. In his hit song "No Woman No Cry," Bob Marley mused, "In this great _____, you can't forget your past."

6. True or false? The word *schwerkraft* is German for "gravity".

7. Who is the author of *Gravity's Rainbow*: Ayn Rand, Thomas Pynchon or William Styron?

8. Who was the last men's tennis player to win a Grand Slam using a wooden racket?

Answers
5. Future   6. True   7. Thomas Pynchon
8. Bjorn Borg (Ken's answer: Rod Laver)

Collect Spinner Books!

ISBN: 1-57528-907-5

ISBN: 1-57528-915-6

ISBN: 1-57528-916-4

ISBN: 1-57528-906-7

ISBN: 1-57528-968-7

ISBN: 1-57528-909-1

Find these books and more at
or your nearest toy store.

UNIVERSITY GAMES 2030 Harrison Street, San Francisco, CA 94110
1-800-347-4818, www.ugames.com